100 SIMPLE SAUCES FOR TODAY'S HEALTHY HOME COOKING

ALSO BY CARL JEROME

Cooking for a New Earth

The Good Health Microwave Book

The Complete Chicken

Recipes for the Cuisinart Food Processor
(with James Beard)

100 SIMPLE SAUCES

·

FOR TODAY'S HEALTHY

·

HOME COOKING

·

Easy-to-Prepare Salsas, Relishes,

Chutneys, Marinades, and Much More

Carl Jerome

An Owl Book

Henry Holt and Company · New York

Henry Holt and Company, Inc.
Publishers since 1866
115 West 18th Street
New York, New York 10011

Henry Holt ® is a registered
trademark of Henry Holt and Company, Inc.

Published in Canada by Fitzhenry & Whiteside Ltd.,
195 Allstate Parkway, Markham, Ontario L3R 4T8.

Library of Congress Cataloging-in-Publication Data
Jerome, Carl.
100 simple sauces for today's healthy home cooking / Carl Jerome.
p.   cm.
"An Owl book."
Includes index.
1. Sauces.   2. Quick and easy cookery.   I. Title.
TX819 .A1 J47   1997   96-44779
641.8'14—dc20   CIP

ISBN 0-8050- 4799-9

Henry Holt books are available for special promotions
and premiums. For details contact: Director, Special Markets.

First Edition—1997

Designed by Betty Lew
Illustrations by Margaret Riegel

Printed in the United States of America
All first editions are printed on acid-free paper. ∞

3   5   7   9   10   8   6   4   2

For Nicholas

Contents

Introduction

Everything you serve will look better and taste better when it's accompanied by one of the hundred modern sauces in this book.

Sauces are the accessories in a modern cook's wardrobe. They can be used to dress up everything from a simple piece of broiled fish to a poached chicken breast or slices of a baked ham. They give color, textural interest, and excitement to vegetarian meals.

The salsas, chutneys, relishes, and salad dressings; the broths, marinades, and dipping sauces; the vegetable, yogurt, barbecue, and fish- and meat-based sauces in this book are so easy to make that most can be thrown together with little more effort than a few minutes of chopping or cutting and a couple of seconds of mixing.

These light, healthy sauces—flavor and texture intense, deeply aromatic, sometimes exotic or transethnic (fusion sauces, as they are sometimes called)—have leaped onto our plates in the last twenty years, largely as a result of the whole-foods and health-foods movement that was started by the counterculture of the 1960s. Nonetheless, several thousand years of culinary history have led to these vibrant and vital sauces, which are becoming part of our everyday cooking.

Three major culinary trends that thread though the history of food are clearly reflected in the way Americans make sauces today. First of all, we are concerned about the relationship between the food we eat and our health. Second, we believe that we are somehow making the food we eat "lighter" than in previous decades and centuries. Third, we have an aesthetic need for simple, pure flavors, on the one hand, and for exotic and dramatic food, on the other.

The early Chinese were the first to understand that there was a direct relationship between the foods we eat and our physical and spiritual health. Like the Chinese, the ancient Greeks closely linked their diet with their medicine. The Greeks also believed in using the finest quality ingredients and in simple flavors and preparations.

The ancient Romans, while closely following the Greek model for cooking and eating, gave us two major innovations in sauce making. They added acids to give the flavor of the sauces better balance, sometimes producing sweet-and-sour sauces; and they thickened sauces, for the first time, with eggs and starches.

During the very early Middle Ages, largely as a result of the Crusades, new and exotic ingredients were introduced into the cooking of Europe, ingredients like pomegranates, saffron, and pistachios. Here we see the beginnings of today's culinary interest in exotic ingredients, transethnic combinations, and brightly colored foods.

During the Renaissance, there was a renewed interest in Greek culture. This led to a major concern with how food affects health, patterned largely on the Greek idea of eating properly so that the four basic bodily fluids, known as *humors* (sanguine, phlegmatic, choleric, and melancholic) could be kept in balance. Other than a dramatic increase in the amount of refined sugar used in cooking and making sauces, culinary aesthetics remained the same during the Renaissance.

In the seventeenth century, however, we see the real beginnings of today's palate. It was during the 1600s that herbs and butter were first used in sauce making, as well as shallots, mushrooms, and even truffles. But most important, this is the century in which the roux (a cooked mixture of flour and butter that for three hundred years would be the primary way of thickening sauces) was introduced and in which stock making was refined and codified.

In the eighteenth century there was an interest in using broths and *jus* or juices as sauces, as well as the first recipes for classic French sauces like béchamel, velouté, and hollandaise. As a result of the French Revolution and the development of restaurants in France, and later throughout Europe, sauce making became standardized during the late eighteenth and early nineteenth centuries.

Antonin Carême, the father of classic French cooking, wrote in detail about the "mother" sauces, as well as introducing and legitimizing mayonnaise and vinaigrettes. It was Carême's belief that, in elaborately systematizing French cooking, he was lightening and thus improving French cooking. In sauce making, for example, Carême championed the use of the roux to add a smooth, velvety texture to sauces, dramatically lightening the texture from sauces of the Renaissance, which were thickened with ground bread crumbs and had an uneven, mealy texture.

The twentieth century begins with Auguste Escoffier "lightening" the recipes of

Carême, making new versions of traditional sauces with little or no flour, and using cream and butter as thickening agents. Ferdinand Point, a student of Escoffier and the most respected French chef of the mid–twentieth century, worked within the new, lighter aesthetic of Escoffier. Point reached out to bring both regional and home cooking ideas and techniques into mainstream commercial cooking, paving the way for the development of *la nouvelle cuisine*—a phrase first used as the title of a book in 1742—in the 1960s.

This innovative and creative "new" cuisine was often international and exotic in inspiration. It was dramatic and colorful in appearance and emphasized, more than ever before, quality ingredients, "lighter" dishes, and intensely flavored sauces that were often made without flour and sometimes made without butter, cream, or eggs.

Michel Guérard, one of the most important and innovative French chefs of the 1970s, integrated *la nouvelle cuisine* with today's health concerns, further lightening modern cooking and sauce making. In doing so, he paved the way for new American sauces and salsa and chutneys, for the flavor-intense, healthy sauces of today, for the kinds of sauces you will find in this book.

My own culinary roots are in the new American/California-style cooking and in classical European cooking. I learned to appreciate today's American cooking while working side by side with James Beard in the early and mid-1970s; I came to value and use classical elements of European (as well as Asian and North African) cuisines while living and studying food in Europe in the late 1970s.

It is this dual background, plus a belief in the need to walk lightly on the planet, that informs the sauce recipes presented here. There are some classical overtones to how the sauces are made and used, but always within a very American aesthetic and preparation style.

I use sauces to make foods more colorful and attractive, and as a way of adding fresh new flavors to a dish to raise it out of the monotony of everyday eating. My classical training leads me to believe that sauces are and always should be an essential part of home cooking.

The sauces in this book are light and easy to prepare. I have designed them so that they can be made in minutes, rather than hours.

NOTES ON USING AND STORING SAUCES AND MARINADES

Sauces that are made from an uncooked combination of ingredients, such as salsas or the Fresh Apple Chutney, should be made and used in the same day. Lightly cooked sauces, which are heated for just a few minutes, can be made a day or two ahead and stored, tightly covered, in the refrigerator. None of these uncooked or barely cooked sauces should be frozen. The remaining sauces in this book, such as many of the tomato and barbecue sauces, can be stored in the refrigerator for up to three days, tightly covered, or frozen for up to three months.

WARNING

A few sauces in this book call for hot peppers like poblanos, jalapeños, serranos, habaneros, and anchos. All hot peppers contain volatile oils that can cause irritation. When you are cleaning and seeding these peppers, wear plastic gloves and don't touch your eyes and nose. As soon after handling the peppers as possible, thoroughly wash your hands, the cutting board, and everything else that has come in contact with the peppers.

HOW TO USE THIS BOOK

Chapters are organized by sauce category, so you can find all the salsas, or all the tomato sauces, in a given chapter and choose the one you want. The appendix, "Food List with Suggested Sauces," allows you to look up, for example, chicken or beef or ham and to find all the suggested sauces for that main ingredient. In addition, there is the usual index.

1

......

VEGETARIAN SAUCES

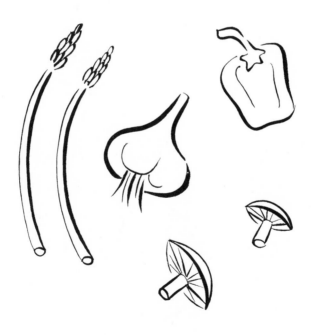

Asparagus Sauce

Black Bean Sauce with Mild Green Chilies
Black Bean Sauce with Fermented Black Beans

Black Bean, Tomato, and Dill Sauce

Pale Pink Bean Sauce

White Bean Aioli
Saffron Aioli
Mustard Aioli

White Bean Sauce
Curried White Bean Sauce
Saffron White Bean Sauce
Rosemary-flavored White Bean Sauce
Light Mustard White Bean Sauce

Traditional Italian Green Sauce

Sesame-Scented Lentil Sauce

Forest Mushroom Sauce

Mushroom and Eggplant Sauce with Tomatoes and Herbs

Jean-Louis Palladin's Incredible Onion Sauce

Poblano and Green Bell Pepper Sauce with Mint

Roasted Red Pepper Purée with Orange and Dill
Chilied Roasted Red Pepper Purée
Roasted Yellow Pepper Purée

Red Pepper Sofrito

Green Pepper Sofrito

A Sprightly Tomatillo Sauce

Wasabi Mustard Sauce

ASPARAGUS SAUCE

This electric-green sauce has a delicate, sweet flavor, gently enhanced by a suggestion of onion, garlic, and rosemary.

Serve cold with vegetables, like asparagus, broccoli, or yellow tomatoes. Use as a dressing for pasta and potato salads, or as a topping for baked potatoes. Serve hot with grilled fish or grilled chicken.
Makes about 2 cups

3 shallots, peeled and finely chopped
1 small garlic clove, finely chopped
Pinch of dried rosemary
1 tablespoon extra-virgin or virgin olive oil

1 pound asparagus, washed under cold running water and cut into 2-inch lengths
Freshly ground black pepper

Place the shallots, garlic, and rosemary in a nonstick sauté pan. Drizzle with the oil and stir around in the pan so that all the shallots and garlic are lightly coated with the oil. Cook over low heat, partially covered, stirring occasionally, until shallots are tender, about 10 minutes.

In the meantime, bring a large saucepan of water to a boil. Add the asparagus and boil until tender, about 4 to 6 minutes. Immediately drain, reserving ½ cup of the cooking water, and cool completely under cold running water to stop the cooking and to set the color. Drain and pat dry.

In a food processor, purée the asparagus with the reserved cooking liquid and the shallots and garlic to form a thick, slightly textured sauce. Taste, then season lightly with pepper.

BLACK BEAN SAUCE WITH
MILD GREEN CHILIES

This dark sauce has a smooth texture and combines the flavors of rich beans and mild chilies.

Serve with nachos or tacos, or other traditional Tex-Mex dishes. Use as a bean dip for chips, or add to risotto or polenta for a non-Italian accent. As a vegetarian sauce, it goes well with steamed mixed vegetables or baked potatoes.

Makes about 3¼ cups

1 15-ounce can black beans, undrained
1 4-ounce can diced mild green chilies, drained
1 cup vegetable or chicken stock
Salt and freshly ground black pepper

Pour the beans and their liquid, the chilies, and the stock into a blender and whirl on high until a very smooth sauce forms, about 60 seconds. Season with salt and pepper to taste. Heat in a small saucepan and serve.

Black Bean Sauce with Fermented Black Beans

Replace the chilies with 3 tablespoons fermented black beans or 3 tablespoons Chinese Black Bean Garlic Sauce (both available in Asian markets).

BLACK BEAN, TOMATO, AND DILL SAUCE

This sprightly summer sauce, with its smooth texture and rich, fresh tastes, takes only 2 or 3 minutes to prepare.

Serve on cold pasta salads. Use as a dip for raw or cooked vegetables; as an accompaniment to cold chicken, fish, or pork; or as a sandwich spread.

Makes about 3 cups

1 15-ounce can black beans, undrained
2 medium vine-ripened tomatoes, cored
   and cut into about 8 pieces each
1 tablespoon balsamic vinegar

1 small bunch (about ½ cup) fresh dill,
   thick stems removed
Freshly ground black pepper

Purée the beans, tomatoes, and vinegar in a blender until very smooth. Add the dill and blend until finely chopped. Taste, then season with pepper.

PALE PINK BEAN SAUCE

Here is a smooth, salmon-pink sauce with a very mild tomato flavor. To add a little kick to it, use hot instead of sweet paprika.

Toss this sauce with fresh fava beans, green beans or haricots verts; or serve on pasta primavera. Use it to thicken stews or to add new oomph to leftover soups.

Makes about 3 cups

1 15-ounce can pink beans, undrained
¾ cup vegetable or chicken stock
½ cup tomato juice
1 teaspoon sweet or hot Hungarian paprika
Salt and freshly ground black pepper

Pour the beans and their liquid, the stock, tomato juice, and paprika into a blender and whirl on high until a very smooth sauce forms, about 60 seconds. Season with salt and pepper to taste. Heat in a small saucepan and serve.

WHITE BEAN AIOLI

Aioli is the robust, garlic-flavored mayonnaise that is used as an everyday condiment in the south of France. In this recipe, a quickly made white bean purée replaces mayonnaise as the base for a light aioli flavored with garlic and lemon.

Serve with roast or grilled lamb, with lamb chops, with cold, poached salmon, or use as a topping for baked potatoes or cold vegetables. Pass with vegetable or fish soups so diners can stir a few tablespoons into their soups. Also makes a fine sandwich spread and dip.

Makes about 1½ cups

> About 1½ cups home-cooked white beans
>   (or 1 16-ounce can, drained)
> 2 to 3 garlic cloves, peeled
> Juice of 1 lemon
> Salt and freshly ground black pepper

In a food processor, purée the beans, garlic, and lemon juice until smooth and creamy. In small batches, scoop the sauce into a strainer and press with the back of a kitchen spoon to push the smooth sauce through, discarding any unsoftened bits of the beans. Season with salt and pepper.

Saffron Aioli

Add to the beans before puréeing either 1 teaspoon saffron threads or 1 teaspoon ground turmeric.

Mustard Aioli

Add 2 tablespoons Dijon mustard and 1 tablespoon of a coarsely cracked mustard to either the White Bean Aioli or Saffron variation above.

WHITE BEAN SAUCE

This beautiful, lightly thickened white bean sauce can substitute for a traditional white sauce, such as a béchamel.

Serve with pasta or steamed or boiled vegetables. Spoon over broiled or poached fish or chicken, or add to casseroles to enrich the flavor.

Makes about 2½ cups

> 1 15-ounce can white beans, undrained
> ½ cup skim milk
> ¾ cup vegetable or chicken stock
> Salt and freshly ground black pepper

Pour the beans and their liquid, the milk, and the stock into a blender and whirl on high until a very smooth sauce forms, about 60 seconds. Season with salt and pepper to taste. Heat in a small saucepan and serve.

Curried White Bean Sauce

Add 2 teaspoons curry powder to the sauce before blending.

Saffron White Bean Sauce

Add ½ teaspoon saffron threads to the sauce before blending.

Rosemary-Flavored White Bean Sauce

Add 2 teaspoons coarsely chopped fresh rosemary (or ½ teaspoon crushed dried rosemary) to the sauce before blending.

Light Mustard White Bean Sauce

Add 2 to 3 tablespoons Dijon (or another mustard of your choice) to the sauce before blending.

TRADITIONAL ITALIAN GREEN SAUCE

One of the boldest-flavored and most versatile green sauces in any cuisine, this Italian favorite appears here in a lightened version with barely a hint of the usual cup or more of olive oil.

Use it to accompany grilled steaks or chops, sautéed or grilled chicken or fish, or steamed fresh vegetables. Also delicious with sausages, boiled meats, and as a condiment to spread on sandwiches.

Makes about 1 cup

2 tablespoons Dijon mustard
2 tablespoons capers
2 garlic cloves
1 ounce (1 tablespoon tightly packed)
   anchovies packed in oil, rinsed well
   under warm running water to remove
   as much of the oil as possible

1 tablespoon olive oil
1 large scallion, trimmed and cut into
   4 to 5 pieces
1½ cups tightly packed fresh parsley
Salt and freshly ground black pepper

In a food processor, process the mustard, capers, garlic, anchovies, oil, and scallion until everything is very well chopped. Add the parsley and process to form a thick but finely chopped sauce. Season with salt and pepper to taste.

SESAME-SCENTED LENTIL SAUCE

This light lentil-flavored sauce is accented by just a few drops of dark sesame oil to complement the naturally complex earthy flavors.

Serve with lamb chops or grilled chicken, or use with pasta. Spoon over steamed asparagus to make an appetizer, or stir into soups or stews to add extra body and dimension to those dishes.

Makes about 3 cups

2 cups canned and drained or home-cooked
    brown or green lentils
1 cup vegetable, chicken, or beef stock
1 teaspoon dark sesame oil
Salt and freshly ground black pepper

In a blender, whirl the lentils, stock, and oil until thoroughly puréed, about 90 seconds. Season with salt and pepper to taste. Bring to a boil in a saucepan placed over medium heat and serve immediately.

Note: The recipe for vegetable stock is on page 85, for chicken stock, page 82, and beef stock page 79.

FOREST MUSHROOM SAUCE

Textured yet tender, this sauce has all the rich colors of late autumn in redwood country and the woodsy flavors of a New England forest.

Serve with beef, lamb, or pork, either grilled, broiled, or roasted. Also with sautéed or poached chicken or with game, such as venison, elk, or moose.

Makes about 2 cups

1 medium onion, finely chopped
1 garlic clove, peeled and finely chopped
2 quarter-size slices fresh gingerroot, peeled and finely chopped
2 teaspoons extra-virgin or virgin olive oil
½ pound cremini mushrooms, halved then thinly sliced

½ pound shiitake mushrooms, halved then thinly sliced
½ pound chanterelle mushrooms, halved then thinly sliced
1 cup dry white wine or stock
1 tablespoon balsamic vinegar
1 tablespoon fresh tarragon, finely chopped

Place the onion, garlic, and ginger in a very large saucepan. Drizzle with the oil and stir around in the pan until all three ingredients are lightly coated with the oil. Cook over low heat, partially covered, stirring occasionally, until the onion is tender, about 10 minutes.

Add the mushrooms and wine or stock and increase the heat to medium. Cover and cook, stirring occasionally, until the mushrooms have wilted down to about half their original volume, about 6 minutes. Uncover and cook over moderately low heat until the mushrooms are very soft and the liquid in the pan evaporates, about 20 to 25 minutes. Remove from the heat and stir in the vinegar and tarragon.

MUSHROOM AND EGGPLANT SAUCE WITH TOMATOES AND HERBS

Thick and chunky, this eggplant sauce is similar to a mushroom ratatouille.

Serve hot over corkscrew, squiggly, or other medium-sized pastas or atop polenta or risotto. Also use cold as a dip or to accompany antipasti. Spoon on roast beef or chicken sandwiches, or drain and stuff into sourdough rolls for a vegetarian sandwich.

Makes about 4 cups

1 ounce dried porcini mushrooms
½ medium onion, finely chopped
1 small garlic clove, finely chopped
1 teaspoon olive or canola oil
1-pound eggplant, ends trimmed and dis-
    carded, then cut into ¼- to ½-inch dice
8 ounces small cultivated mushrooms,
    each cut into sixths like a pie

2 large vine-ripened tomatoes or 2 cups
    diced Italian-style plum tomatoes in
    purée
1 tablespoon fresh parsley, finely chopped
6 large basil leaves, neatly stacked atop
    each other, then cut into fine shreds
1 tablespoon sherry vinegar
Salt and freshly ground black pepper

Place the dried mushrooms in 1 cup boiling water and set aside for 5 minutes. Drain, reserving the liquid, and cut any large mushroom pieces in half. Set aside in a small bowl. Pour the reserved liquid through a strainer lined with a paper towel, then combine with the mushrooms. Set aside.

In a large microwave-safe bowl, combine the onion and garlic and mix well with the oil. Cover tightly and microwave on high (100 percent) for 3 minutes. Carefully uncover and add the reserved dried mushrooms and their liquid, the eggplant, cultivated mushrooms, and toma-toes. Cover and microwave on high for 25 minutes.

Stir very well so the sauce forms a thick, homogeneous mixture, then toss in the herbs and vinegar, and season with salt and pepper to taste.

JEAN-LOUIS PALLADIN'S
INCREDIBLE ONION SAUCE

With its smooth texture and delicate, sweet onion flavor, this is an exceptionally versatile sauce. It was created by one of the greatest chefs in the United States, Jean-Louis Palladin, owner of Jean-Louis at the Watergate in Washington, D.C.

Serve with poached, broiled, or roasted chicken; atop any kind of poached, steamed, or baking fish; or spooned over vegetables or pasta.

Makes about 1 ½ cups

> **1 pound sweet onions, such as Vidalia**
> **¼ teaspoon turmeric**
> **½ cup vegetable or chicken stock**
> **2 teaspoons olive oil**
> **Salt and freshly ground black pepper**

In a large microwave-safe bowl, combine the onions, turmeric, and ¼ cup of the stock. Seal tightly with plastic film and microwave on high (100 percent) for 10 minutes or until the onions are very tender.

In the jar of a blender, combine the cooked onions with their cooking liquid, the remaining stock and oil, and cover securely. Hold a thick towel over the cover to prevent the sauce from spewing out all over the kitchen, and purée on high until very smooth.

Pour into a fine strainer, pressing to force as much of the sauce through as possible. Season with salt and pepper to taste.

Poblano and Green Bell Pepper Sauce with Mint

This speckled, pistachio-green sauce has a fresh green pepper flavor, a tangy hotness, and the aroma of a newly mowed lawn. The sauce is light and frothy, yet highly textured. It is best made just before serving. Follow the precautions on page xiv for seeding hot peppers.

Serve with steamed or boiled vegetables, as a dressing for tomato slices or coleslaw, or as a topping for baked potatoes. Adds zest to sautéed or grilled fish, grilled chicken, broiled or grilled pork chops or lamb chops. Makes a good pasta sauce as well.

Makes about 2 cups

12 ounces (3 medium) poblanos, cored, seeded, and cut into 8 pieces each

12 ounces (2 medium) green bell peppers, cored, seeded, and cut into 8 pieces each

2 tablespoons fresh mint, dill, or cilantro, coarsely chopped

Salt

Microwave the poblanos and bell peppers in a tightly covered bowl for 5 minutes 30 seconds on high (100 percent). Cool completely under cold running water to stop the cooking and to set the color. Drain and pat dry.

In a food processor, purée the cooked peppers with the herb until a liquidy sauce forms. Taste, then season lightly with salt.

To serve hot, reheat in a saucepan over medium-high heat, stirring frequently; to serve cold, place in a tightly covered container and refrigerate until needed.

ROASTED RED PEPPER PURÉE WITH ORANGE AND DILL

This delicately textured sauce has a deep salmon color and combines the flavors of rich, sweet peppers and fresh dill.

Serve with grilled or sautéed fish, especially tuna, swordfish, or salmon, or with poached or grilled chicken breasts. Spoon over steamed vegetables, such as asparagus and broccoli, or over baked winter squashes.

Makes about 2 cups

> **4 large red bell peppers**
> **Juice of ½ orange**
> **1 tablespoon fresh dill**

Arrange the peppers, evenly spaced, in a foil-lined roasting pan. Slide onto a rack so that the peppers are about 3 inches from the broiling unit. Broil until the skins of the peppers are completely black, turning as needed so that the skins char evenly. This can take as long as 30 minutes.

Carefully transfer the peppers to a thick plastic bag and seal. The peppers will steam as they cool, making them easy to peel. When cool, carefully peel off the charred skin, trying not to tear the peppers. Remove the stems and seeds. If necessary, rinse quickly under cold running water.

In a food processor, purée with the orange juice until a finely textured sauce forms. Add the dill and pulse until it is finely chopped.

Chilied Roasted Red Pepper Purée

Substitute 1 tablespoon Homemade Chili Powder (page 100) or store-bought chili powder for the dill.

Roasted Yellow Pepper Purée

Substitute yellow bell peppers for the red, and chives for the dill.

RED PEPPER SOFRITO

This is a fire-engine red, chunky-textured tomato, onion, garlic, and cumin flavored sofrito—a condiment in Central and South American cooking used much like ketchup is used in American cooking.

Use as a flavoring agent by adding to soups and stews, pasta dishes, and risottos. Also as a sauce over grilled lamb chops or grilled or sautéed salmon, swordfish, sturgeon, or shark.

Makes 2 cups

2 red bell peppers, finely chopped
1 large ripe tomato, finely chopped
½ small red onion, finely chopped
2 large garlic cloves, finely chopped

2 teaspoons olive or canola oil
2 teaspoons ground cumin
Salt and freshly ground black pepper

Combine everything in a saucepan, stir well, and bring to a boil over medium heat. Reduce the heat and simmer for 5 minutes. Season with salt and pepper to taste.

GREEN PEPPER SOFRITO

This green variation on the traditional Red Pepper Sofrito (page 16) is full of bright herb flavors.

Add to soups and stews, use with risotto or polenta, or serve as a sauce over grilled pork chops or chicken breasts.

Makes 2 cups

3 large green bell peppers, finely chopped

5 thin scallions, trimmed and finely
  chopped

2 large garlic cloves, finely chopped

2 teaspoons olive oil

½ teaspoon crushed dried rosemary

½ teaspoon crushed dried thyme

½ cup fresh parsley, finely chopped

½ cup fresh dill, finely chopped

Grated zest of 1 lime

Salt and freshly ground black pepper

Combine everything in a saucepan, stir well, and bring to a boil over medium heat. Reduce the heat and simmer for 5 minutes. Season with salt and pepper to taste.

A Sprightly Tomatillo Sauce

With its very slightly coarse texture and its gentle acidic flavor from the green tree tomatoes (tomatillos), as well as hints of onion, garlic, jalapeño, and herbs, this is a sauce to brighten up any meal—Mexican, Tex-Mex, or whatever.

Tastes great with enchiladas or empanadas, with tacos or nachos, or use as a dipping sauce for cooked or raw fresh vegetables. Serve alongside well-seasoned grilled pork chops or rich fish, like tuna and swordfish.

Makes about 2½ cups

16 ounces tomatillos, husked, stemmed, and quartered

½ green bell pepper, stemmed, cored, and quartered

½ small jalapeño, seeded

2 large garlic cloves

2 scallions, trimmed and cut into 4 to 5 pieces each

½ cup fresh parsley leaves

½ cup cilantro leaves

Salt and freshly ground black pepper

In a food processor, combine the tomatillos, green pepper, jalapeño, garlic, scallions, parsley, and cilantro and purée until a very fine sauce forms. Season with salt and pepper to taste.

WASABI MUSTARD SAUCE

This new mustard sauce is for those who love the intense flavor of wasabi, the Japanese horseradish that is served with sushi and sashami.

Serve alongside steaks or chops or with cold grilled fish. Use with sushi in place of the traditional wasabi paste. If spread discreetly, this mustard sauce can be used on leftover sliced or shaved ham or roast beef.

Makes about ⅔ cup

½ cup Dijon mustard
1 tablespoon Japanese wasabi powder
2 tablespoons fresh dill, finely chopped
¼ teaspoon freshly ground black pepper

Mix everything together. Can be refrigerated in a covered jar for up to 1 month.

2

......

CHUTNEYS, RELISHES, AND GREMOLATAS

The lines that once defined the differences between a chutney and a relish have blurred considerably in the last two decades as chefs and food writers have defined new ways of making these condiments. Traditionally, chutneys were cooked until tender, chunky, spicy, and acidic; relishes were cooked or uncooked, finely textured, and highly acidic. Today, chutneys are generally lighter and fresher tasting, made with shorter cooking times and fewer spices or acids; relishes are finer, more highly textured, and less acidic.

Gremolatas are intensely flavored garnishes. Like chutneys and relishes, they complement and enhance a dish through intense contrast. Traditionally, gremolatas were used only with Italian stews. The gremolatas included here come in a variety of flavors, ranging from herb to fruit, which greatly expands the possibilities for using these garnishes.

The recommended serving size is about 3 tablespoons of chutney, 1 to 2 tablespoons of relish, and 1 teaspoon of gremolata.

CHUTNEYS

Fresh Apple Chutney

Holiday Three-Berry and Beet Chutney

Pear and Red Wine Chutney

Red Cabbage and Raspberry Chutney

Many Vegetable Chutney

RELISHES

Confetti Relish

Sweet-and-Sour Corn Relish

Golden Beet Relish

Green Bell Pepper and Dill Relish

Hot-and-Wet Thai-Style Uncooked Relish

GREMOLATAS

Cilantro and Jalapeño Gremolata

Green Peppercorn and Dill Gremolata

Parsley, Tarragon, Red Onion, and Lemon Gremolata

Dried Apricot, Currant, and Orange Gremolata

Dried Blueberry, Lemon, and Candied Pineapple Gremolata

Dried Cherry and Cranberry Gremolata

FRESH APPLE CHUTNEY

Full of crisp textures, with just the right balance of sweetness and tartness, this slightly mint-flavored chutney is one of my favorites.

Serve with baked ham, roasted turkey, or grilled or roasted lamb. Also, spoon onto biscuits, pancakes, or French toast.

Makes about 2 cups

1 large Granny Smith apple, stemmed, cored, and cut into 1- to 2-inch chunks

2 tablespoons golden raisins

1 small celery rib, cut into 5 to 6 pieces

½ cup watercress leaves

1 to 1½ tablespoons tightly packed fresh mint leaves

Juice of ½ lemon

Salt and freshly ground black pepper

In a food processor, combine the apple, raisins, celery, watercress, mint, and lemon juice. Pulse rapidly until a coarsely chopped chutney forms. Season with salt and pepper to taste.

Holiday Three-Berry and Beet Chutney

This sweet, fresh-tasting berry compote is made from frozen berries rather than fresh so it can be enjoyed all winter. The sauce is sweet and fruity with subtle vegetable flavorings. The beets add color and smoothness.

Serve with turkey, goose, or ham for Thanksgiving or Christmas dinner, or with grilled or roasted chicken or capon anytime. Use as a sandwich spread or to accompany steamed or boiled vegetables.
Makes about 2 cups

1 medium red onion, peeled and quartered
1 large raw beet, peeled and quartered
2-inch piece fresh gingerroot, peeled and cut into 3 pieces
2 large garlic cloves, peeled
Juice of 1 large orange
⅓ cup sugar
2 cups (about 12 ounces by weight) unsweetened, individually frozen raspberries

1 cup (about 6 ounces by weight) unsweetened, individually frozen blackberries
1 cup (about 6 ounces by weight) unsweetened, individually frozen blueberries or dark, sweet cherries
Grated zest of 1 lemon
Freshly ground black pepper

In a food processor, combine the onion, beet, ginger, and garlic and pulse until finely chopped. Transfer to a large saucepan and stir in the orange juice, sugar, and berries. Bring to a boil over medium heat, then reduce the heat and simmer, partially covered, for 10 minutes. Uncover and simmer until most of the liquid has evaporated and a thick sauce has formed, about 20 minutes more.

PEAR AND RED WINE CHUTNEY

Luscious tender pears are glazed in a gently spiced syrup of red wine and raspberries to make this chutney, which is full-bodied and rich in the flavors of autumn.

Serve with roast pork or chicken. Spoon over ham, steaks, pancakes, or French toast. Double or triple the recipe and use as a condiment for Thanksgiving, Christmas, or New Year's dinner.

Makes about 4 cups

1½ cups merlot
⅓ cup sugar
¼ small lemon
¾ cup frozen raspberries

8 medium ripe Comise pears, peeled, cored, and cut into ¼-inch dice
1 stick cinnamon

Pour the wine into a large nonreactive saucepan and add the sugar, lemon, and raspberries. Bring to a boil, stirring occasionally to dissolve the sugar, then reduce the heat and simmer for 10 minutes. Strain, discarding the berry pulp and returning the red wine to the saucepan. Bring back to a boil, add the pears, reduce the heat, and simmer until pears are very tender, about 3 to 5 minutes.

With a slotted spoon, transfer the pears to a heat-resistant bowl and set aside. Add the cinnamon stick to the red wine and boil gently until reduced to ½ cup. As the wine reduces, it will thicken and bubble up, so be certain the saucepan holds at least 2 quarts. Remove and discard the cinnamon stick. Pour red wine reduction over the pears and chill until needed.

RED CABBAGE AND RASPBERRY CHUTNEY

This deep fuchsia–colored chutney has the sweet texture and flavor of slow-cooked red cabbage with an unexpectedly heady raspberry fragrance counterbalanced by a little fruit vinegar.

Serve with roasted pork or turkey, or with grilled lamb chops. Spoon over green beans or broccoli, or spread on turkey, cheese, or vegetarian sandwiches.

Makes about 2½ cups

1 pound (half a small red cabbage), cut into 6 to 8 chunks
1 small red onion, quartered
1 10-ounce package raspberries in syrup, defrosted
2 tablespoons raspberry vinegar
Salt and freshly ground black pepper

In a food processor, combine the cabbage, onion, and the raspberries with their syrup. Pulse until the cabbage is finely chopped. Transfer to a large pot and bring to a boil over medium heat, stirring occasionally. Partially cover pot, reduce the heat and simmer, stirring occasionally, until cabbage is just tender, about 45 minutes. Turn off the heat, stir in the vinegar, and season with salt and pepper.

MANY VEGETABLE CHUTNEY

Here is a richly textured, brightly colored chutney with a hint of curry. The secret to this sauce, created by a former student, Charles Kirschner, is to cut all the vegetables into neat quarter-inch dice so they can meld in the cooking process to form a new single taste that is both subtle and complex.

Serve with grilled marinated chicken, glazed ham, or with seared or broiled fresh salmon or tuna. Spoon on curried lamb or chicken, or spread on sandwiches.

Makes 3 cups

1 medium tart green apple, cut into ¼-inch dice

Juice of ½ lemon

1 medium carrot, cut into ¼-inch dice

½ medium yellow onion, cut into small dice

2 garlic cloves, finely chopped

1 medium red bell pepper, cut into ¼-inch dice

2 tablespoons canola or olive oil

1 medium zucchini, cut into ¼-inch dice

1 medium yellow (crookneck) squash, cut into ¼-inch dice

2 tablespoons mango chutney (sometimes called Major Grey chutney)

½ teaspoon curry powder

⅛ teaspoon each ground coriander, cardamom, and white pepper

¼ cup chopped walnuts

3 tablespoons currants

¼ teaspoon kosher or sea salt

Toss the apple and lemon juice together and set aside. In a large saucepan, mix the carrot, onion, garlic, and red pepper with the oil. Cover and cook over low heat until carrots are just tender, about 8 to 10 minutes. Stir in the zucchini and yellow squash, cover, and cook until squashes are tender, about 2 minutes. Stir in the spices, walnuts, and currants and cook for 1 minute longer. Add the apple, drained of any juice, and season with salt to taste. Serve warm or at room temperature.

CONFETTI RELISH

Made from 4 different-colored sweet bell peppers and eggplant, all cut into tiny dice the size of pieces of old-fashioned confetti, this festive relish is reminiscent of the flavors of ratatouille.

Serve over broiled or grilled chicken, or with roasted pork or ham or turkey. Stir a couple of spoonfuls into leftover soups to give them new life. Also goes well with beef stews.

Makes about 4 cups

1 red bell pepper, cored, seeded, cut into thin strips, then into tiny dice

1 green bell pepper, cored, seeded, cut into thin strips, then into tiny dice

1 yellow bell pepper, cored, seeded, cut into thin strips, then into tiny dice

1 orange bell pepper, cored, seeded, cut into thin strips, then into tiny dice

½ small eggplant, the skin cut into strips like the peppers, then into tiny dice

Pinch of crushed dried marjoram

Pinch of crushed dried thyme

Pinch of crushed dried rosemary

½ cup V-8 juice

Salt and freshly ground black pepper

Combine all the ingredients in a large heavy-bottomed saucepan and bring to a boil over medium heat. Reduce the heat and simmer until vegetables are just barely tender, about 5 to 8 minutes. Season with salt and pepper to taste. Serve hot.

SWEET-AND-SOUR CORN RELISH

This colorful, intensely textured and flavored corn relish is a winter staple in my kitchen. Make it in summer or early fall when fresh local corn is available.

Serve as an accent with almost any leftover—chicken, turkey, fish, lamb, or steamed vegetables. Use for Thanksgiving or Christmas dinner, or to enliven simpler family meals.

Makes about 4 cups

5 ears sweet yellow corn
½ cup green bell pepper, finely chopped
½ cup red bell pepper, finely chopped
½ cup celery, finely chopped
½ cup yellow onion, finely chopped
½ cup sugar

1¼ teaspoons pickling salt or kosher salt
1¼ teaspoons mustard seed
1¼ teaspoons celery seed
¾ cup white wine vinegar or tarragon
  vinegar

Shuck the corn and with a sharp knife, cut the kernels off the stalks. There will be about 4 to 5 cups. Mix with the peppers, celery, and onion.

In a large nonaluminum pot, bring to a boil the sugar, pickling salt, mustard seed, celery seed, and vinegar, stirring until the sugar is dissolved. Add the corn mixture, bring back to a boil, reduce the heat, and simmer for 5 minutes. Cover and set aside until cooled.

Ladle 1 cup relish into a jar and refrigerate for current use. The remainder can be placed in plastic freezer bags and frozen for up to 3 months.

GOLDEN BEET RELISH

With its long shreds from grating and its goldenrod color, this mildest of beets makes a sweet, friendly relish with hints of orange and sherry.

Serve with grilled lamb or veal chops, or with firm-fleshed and rich fish, like mahimahi, monkfish, lingcod, salmon, tuna, or sturgeon; or use to add festiveness to holiday hams and turkeys.

Makes about 2 cups

3 large golden beets
Juice and finely grated zest of 1 orange
1 tablespoon sherry vinegar
Salt and freshly ground black pepper

Trim off the ends without cutting into the beet. Place in a microwave-safe bowl, cover with plastic film, and microwave on high (100 percent) until tender when pierced with a fork, about 4 to 5 minutes. (Alternatively, boil the beet until tender.) Cool then grate coarsely.

Combine the beets with the orange juice and zest, and the sherry vinegar. Season with salt and pepper to taste. Refrigerate until needed.

Green Bell Pepper and Dill Relish

This barely cooked, slightly textured relish can be made fresh in winter, for it is full of cold-weather flavors, like sweet green peppers and dill.

Serve with grilled, broiled, or roasted chicken; use as a topping for chicken or fish enchiladas; or pass alongside roasted or grilled lamb.

Makes about 2½ cups

2 large green bell peppers, cored and
   seeded and cut into 1- to 2-inch chunks
1 large shallot, quartered
1 large garlic clove
1 teaspoon celery seed
¼ cup fresh parsley, finely chopped

½ cup fresh dill, finely chopped
1 teaspoon dried tarragon, crushed
1½ tablespoons white wine or tarragon
   vinegar
Salt and freshly ground black pepper

In a food processor, combine the peppers, shallot, garlic, and celery seed and pulse rapidly until everything is finely chopped and a liquidy, bright green sauce forms.

Transfer to a saucepan and boil over medium heat until virtually all the visible liquid has evaporated, about 5 minutes. Cool to room temperature, then add the parsley, dill, tarragon, and vinegar. Season with salt and pepper to taste.

Hot-and-Wet Thai-Style Uncooked Relish

This relish is wet and cool while also a little hot and spicy.

It goes well with grilled, baked, or broiled light-flavored fish, like halibut or cod, or with chicken.

Makes about 1½ cups

2 celery ribs, washed and cut into
   1-inch pieces
1 very large cucumber, peeled, seeded,
   and cut into 1-inch pieces
½ cup parsley leaves
1-inch-long, thick piece fresh gingerroot,
   peeled and cut into 4 pieces

1 large garlic clove
¼ small hot chili pepper
Juice of 1 lime
2 tablespoons nam pla (Thai fish sauce,
   available at Asian grocers)
Big pinch of freshly ground black pepper

Combine all the ingredients in the bowl of a food processor and pulse until they are finely chopped. Serve refrigerator cold.

CILANTRO AND JALAPEÑO GREMOLATA

This is a gremolata with Central and South American flavors.

Gently sprinkle over nachos or sliced roasted lamb; stir into stews and soups; or mix into salad dressings.

Makes ⅓ cup

¼ cup finely chopped cilantro
2 teaspoons finely chopped fresh rosemary
   or ½ teaspoon crushed dried rosemary
Finely grated zest of 1 lime

¼ teaspoon celery seed
½ very small jalapeño, seeded, cored, and
   finely chopped
Big pinch of freshly ground black pepper

Mix everything together. Can be refrigerated in a tightly covered jar for 1 to 2 days.

Green Peppercorn and Dill Gremolata

This peppery, intensely herbed gremolata adds vibrancy to simple stews and other winter dishes.

Serve gently sprinkled in winter stews or with grilled steaks. The dill makes this gremolata an excellent choice for rich and full-flavored fish, like sturgeon and swordfish.

Makes ⅓ cup

> 2 teaspoons green peppercorns (from a can or
>   jar, packed in brine or water), drained and
>   either crushed in a mortar or finely chopped
> Finely grated zest of 1 lime
> ½ teaspoon lime juice
> ¼ cup finely chopped dill

Mix everything together. Can be refrigerated in a tightly covered jar for 1 to 2 days.

PARSLEY, TARRAGON, RED ONION, AND LEMON GREMOLATA

This gremolata has a bright parsley flavor with hints of tarragon and a lot of lemon.

Sprinkle over chicken, beef, or lamb stews, or stir about ½ teaspoon into a bowl of soup. Use as a garnish atop polenta or stir a small amount into a risotto.

Makes ⅓ cup

2 tablespoons parsley, finely chopped
1 tablespoon fresh tarragon, finely chopped
2 tablespoons red onion, finely chopped
Finely grated zest of ½ lemon
Big pinch of freshly ground black pepper

Mix everything together. Can be refrigerated in a tightly covered jar for 1 to 2 days.

DRIED APRICOT, CURRANT, AND ORANGE GREMOLATA

This apricot-orange gremolata will add a bright pumpkin color to any food.

Serve with poached fruits, or sprinkle on muffins before baking. At breakfast, pour over pancakes, waffles, or French toast, or stir into hot or cold cereals.

Makes 1¼ cups

> ¾ **cup dried apricots**
> ¼ **cup currants**
> ¼ **cup candied orange peel**

Combine the apricots, currants, and orange peel in a food processor and pulse until finely chopped. Refrigerate until needed.

DRIED BLUEBERRY, LEMON, AND CANDIED PINEAPPLE GREMOLATA

This blue-black sauce is slightly dry and slightly sticky. Its granular texture comes from the addition of shreds of pineapple and bits of lemon zest. It is sweet and intensely flavored, so use it sparingly.

Serve with poached fruits, or sprinkle on pound cakes. At breakfast, spoon a little on pancakes, waffles, or French toast, or stir into hot or cold cereals.

Makes 1½ cups

1 cup dried blueberries
½ cup candied pineapple
Finely grated zest of 1 small lemon

Combine the blueberries and pineapple in a food processor and pulse until finely chopped. Stir in the zest and refrigerate until needed.

DRIED CHERRY AND CRANBERRY GREMOLATA

This is a crimson-colored gremolata boldly flavored with dried cherries and cranberries, enhanced by candied orange peel and grated orange zest.

Serve alongside holiday roasted turkey or ham. At breakfast, use as a light topping for waffles, pancakes, or French toast; or toss into hot cereals.

Makes 2 cups

> 1 cup dried sweet Bing cherries
> ½ cup dried cranberries
> ½ cup diced candied orange peel
> Finely grated zest of ½ orange

Combine the cherries, cranberries, and orange peel in a food processor and pulse until finely chopped. Stir in the zest and refrigerate until needed.

3

......

SALSAS

Salsas are sauces that are generally modeled after the chunky uncooked tomato salsas of Mexico. Often flavored with herbs or hot peppers, they tend to have a lively taste. Traditionally, salsas are made with just vegetables, but many of today's salsas use tropical fruits as well.

Blueberry and Blackberry Orange Salsa

Honeydew and Tomatillo Salsa

Fresh Mango Salsa

Pineapple Salsa

Fresh Raspberry and Beet Salsa

The Best-Ever Tomato Salsa

Fresh Tomato Salsa

Fresh Tomato Salsa with Avocado

Yellow Tomato and Ginger Salsa

BLUEBERRY AND BLACKBERRY ORANGE SALSA

This gently textured, slightly chunky, deeply colored salsa has a fruity aroma.

Serve this sauce with sliced, roasted pork, with broiled or grilled chicken, with grilled tuna or sword-fish. It is also excellent with holiday hams and turkeys.

Makes about 2 cups

½ cup fresh blueberries, finely chopped
½ cup blackberries, finely chopped
½ jalapeño, cored, seeded, and finely chopped (optional)
1 tablespoon red onion, finely chopped
1 tablespoon chives, finely chopped
1 tablespoon cilantro, finely chopped

1 tablespoon fresh parsley, finely chopped
1 teaspoon orange zest, finely grated
1 teaspoon lemon zest, finely grated
2 tablespoons freshly squeezed orange juice
Salt and freshly ground black pepper to taste

Gently stir everything together.

HONEYDEW AND TOMATILLO SALSA

Light and refreshing, this delicately colored salsa is sweet, with a hint of hotness.

Serve with fresh fruits and fruit salads, poached white fish, such as red snapper, striped bass, or halibut, or with grilled or broiled chicken breasts.

Makes about 2 cups

¼ medium honeydew, peeled, seeded, and cut into ¼-inch dice (about 1½ cups)

½ small cucumber, ends trimmed and discarded, peeled, seeded, and cut into ¼-inch dice

2 tomatillos, husks removed, and cut into ¼-inch dice

½ jalapeño, seeds removed, finely chopped (optional)

Juice of 1 lime

3 tablespoons fresh tarragon or mint, finely chopped

Freshly ground black pepper to taste

Mix everything together. Taste, and adjust the flavoring. Add more jalapeño for a hotter salsa.

FRESH MANGO SALSA

Sweet and gingery, full-bodied and fruity, this fresh mango salsa will enliven even the simplest of entrées.
Serve with poached, grilled, or roasted chicken, grilled tuna or salmon, or with duck. A teaspoon of chili powder can be added to the salsa if used with game birds or venison.
Makes about 1 ½ cups

2 large mangoes, peeled and cut into
   medium-size dice
1 tablespoon fresh gingerroot, finely chopped
1 tablespoon balsamic vinegar
Freshly ground black pepper

Mix together the mango, ginger, and vinegar. Add a hint of black pepper.

PINEAPPLE SALSA

This pale yellow salsa has a subtle pineapple flavor with hints of shallot, ginger, and basil, all gently sweetened with honey.

Serve with poached, grilled, or sautéed fish, especially tuna, swordfish, or salmon. Goes well with poached or grilled chicken breasts and, of course, baked ham.

Makes about 3 cups

½ small pineapple, peeled thickly to remove the skin and "eyes," core cut away, then chopped well to form a loose saucelike texture (save the juices that accumulate under the pineapple during chopping)

1 medium yellow tomato, peeled, seeded, and finely diced

1 tablespoon fresh gingerroot, peeled and finely chopped

1 shallot, peeled and finely chopped

Juice of ½ lime

1 tablespoon honey

1 tablespoon fresh basil, finely chopped

¼ teaspoon saffron or ½ teaspoon turmeric (dissolved in 2 tablespoons of the juice that accumulated under the pineapple during chopping)

Mix everything together.

FRESH RASPBERRY AND BEET SALSA

This bright red sauce is a perfect balance of sweet and sour flavors with a bold raspberry aroma.

Serve with roasted pork or lamb, with grilled pork chops or lamb chops, or with duck. Pass alongside sliced holiday ham or roasted turkey.

Makes about 2 cups

1 medium red beet
½ pint (6 ounces) fresh raspberries,
   coarsely chopped
1 tablespoon red onion, finely chopped

1 tablespoon light brown sugar
1 tablespoon raspberry vinegar
1 tablespoon freshly squeezed orange juice
Salt and freshly ground black pepper

Trim off the ends without cutting into the beet. Place in a microwave-safe bowl, cover with plastic film, and microwave on high until tender when pierced with a fork, about 4 to 5 minutes. (Alternatively, boil the beet until tender.) Cool, then grate finely.

Combine the beet with the raspberries, onion, sugar, vinegar, and orange juice. Season with salt and pepper to taste. Refrigerate until needed.

THE BEST-EVER TOMATO SALSA

With its incredible variety of textures and flavors, this mildly hot salsa is certainly one of the greatest tomato salsas ever. Follow the precautions on page xiv for seeding peppers.

Serve with homemade Tex-Mex dishes, on fish steaks like halibut and salmon, as a dip, or pass with grilled or broiled chops or steaks.

Makes about 4 cups

1 large red bell pepper
½ fresh poblano pepper
1 cucumber, peeled, seeded, and finely grated
8 plum tomatoes, peeled, seeded, and finely chopped
1 scallion, finely chopped
1 garlic clove, finely chopped

1 tablespoon fresh parsley, finely chopped
1 tablespoon fresh basil, finely chopped
1 tablespoon fresh cilantro, finely chopped
1 cup tomato juice
2 tablespoons rice vinegar
1 tablespoon balsamic vinegar
1 teaspoon chili powder
Salt and freshly ground black pepper

Place the red pepper and the poblano on a foil-lined roasting pan and slide under a preheated broiling unit. Cook, turning every 5 to 10 minutes, until the peppers are completely and evenly charred. Using tongs, hold the peppers under cold running water to cool them, then peel off all the charred skin, rinsing the peppers in the cold running water as needed. Pat the peppers dry, then remove the stems, core, and seeds. Cut into fine dice.

Combine the peppers with all the other ingredients in a large bowl and mix well. Season with salt and pepper to taste and chill thoroughly.

FRESH TOMATO SALSA

Beefsteak or heirloom tomatoes add a chunkiness to this salsa that supports a good deal of onion flavor and the taste of two herbs, and a hot pepper.

Serve with Tex-Mex and Mexican meals or alongside grilled cheese sandwiches. Spoon over grilled salmon filets, roasted lamb or beef, or steaks.

Makes about 2 cups

2 very large vine-ripened beefsteak or heirloom tomatoes, cored and diced

2 garlic cloves, finely diced

3 thin scallions, white part only, finely chopped

½ cup cilantro, finely chopped

½ cup fresh parsley, finely chopped

Juice of 1 lime

2 tablespoons of a cored and seeded poblano pepper, finely chopped

Salt and freshly ground black pepper

Stir together the tomatoes, garlic, scallions, cilantro, parsley, lime juice, and poblano. Season with salt and pepper to taste.

Fresh Tomato Salsa with Avocado

Here is a simple, utterly fresh, easy-to-make salsa with lots of crisp flavors from the garlic, the jalapeño, and the lemon and lime. The avocado gives the salsa an unexpected softness and richness.

Serve with sautéed chicken or fish, with chips and a light sour cream with most Tex-Mex dishes, or to accompany a plate of mixed spring vegetables. Pour over asparagus, or stir into rice for a Tex-Mex version of Spanish rice.

Makes about 2 cups

2 very large ripe tomatoes, cored, seeded, and coarsely chopped (reserve the juices from the chopping)

1 large garlic clove, finely chopped

½ small jalapeño, stemmed, cored, seeded, and finely chopped

1 tablespoon red onion, finely chopped

½ ripe avocado, peeled, seeded, and coarsely chopped

½ cup cilantro leaves, finely chopped

Juice of 1 lime or ½ lemon

Salt and freshly ground black pepper

Stir together the tomato and its juices, the garlic, jalapeño, onion, avocado, cilantro, and lime or lemon juice. Season with salt and pepper to taste.

YELLOW TOMATO AND GINGER SALSA

This golden orange salsa has a sweet tomato flavor with intense accents of ginger and sherry vinegar. It is an elegant and exciting variation on the traditional red tomato salsa.

Serve with lightly flavored grilled fish, like cod or halibut, or with grilled or broiled chicken breasts or grilled vegetables.

Makes about 2 cups

2 large yellow vine-ripened tomatoes, cored and finely diced
1 large garlic clove, finely chopped
2-inch piece fresh gingerroot, finely grated

2 small shallots, finely chopped
1 tablespoon sherry vinegar
Salt and freshly ground black pepper

Gently stir together the tomato, garlic, ginger, shallot, and sherry vinegar. Season with salt and pepper to taste.

4

......

TOMATO SAUCES

A Very Light Tomato Sauce with Chickpeas

Cocktail Sauce

Fresh Tomato Couli

Ketchup

Marinara Sauce

Puttanesca Sauce

Raw Tomato Concassée

Fresh Italian Ragu

Extra-Easy Sundried Tomato Sauce

Sundried Tomato and Dill Mustard Sauce
Sundried Tomato, Garlic, and Parsley Mustard Sauce

Virgin Bloody Mary Sauce

Yellow Pepper Tomato Sauce

A Very Light Tomato Sauce
with Chickpeas

*This delicate salmon-colored sauce has a very light, fresh tomato flavor that is softened by the chickpeas.
Serve with chicken, pork, or veal, or with sweet-flavored white fishes, like halibut and cod. Pour over
small dried pasta, like rotini, fusilli, shells, or any of the assorted tubular pastas, like penne.*
Makes about 1 ½ cups

1 cup seeded and chopped tomatoes,
either fresh or canned and drained

1 cup cooked chickpeas, either
home-cooked or canned and drained

2 tablespoons fresh parsley leaves
Freshly ground black pepper
1 tablespoon red wine vinegar, if needed

Put the tomatoes, chickpeas, parsley, and a little pepper in a blender, and blend until a sauce forms. Taste, and add vinegar if you wish.

COCKTAIL SAUCE

Here is an exemplary version of the classic, with an exceptional balance of flavors.

Serve this sauce with boiled shrimp, crabmeat just out of the shell, or oysters on the half shell.

Makes about 1½ cups

1½ cups ketchup
1 tablespoon Fresh Horseradish
(page 92) or store-bought horseradish
Juice of ½ lemon
¾ teaspoon Hot Red Pepper Sauce
(page 104) or store-bought pepper sauce

2 garlic cloves
1 thin scallion, trimmed and cut into
4 to 5 pieces
Salt and freshly ground black pepper

In a food processor, combine the ketchup, horseradish, lemon juice, hot pepper sauce, garlic, and scallion and process until the mixture is smooth and the scallions are virtually invisible. Season with salt and pepper to taste. Can be stored in a tightly covered jar in the refrigerator for up to 3 weeks.

FRESH TOMATO COULI

This is a fresh-tasting, gently textured tomato sauce. The shallots and garlic melt into the sauce, and the tomatoes are only cooked long enough to remove their rawness. The final enrichment with balsamic vinegar and fresh parsley gives the sauce an added sprightliness.

Serve with turkey, goose, or ham for Thanksgiving or Christmas dinner, or with grilled or roasted chicken or capon. Use on pastas of all kinds, from thick to thin spaghettis, and from bow ties to shells.
Makes about 2 cups

1 large shallot, peeled and finely chopped
1 garlic clove, peeled and finely chopped
1 teaspoon extra-virgin or virgin olive oil
3 large, meaty, vine-ripened tomatoes, cored, halved horizontally, and squeezed to remove the seeds, then cut into ¼-inch dice

1 tablespoon fresh parsley, finely chopped
1 tablespoon balsamic vinegar
Salt and freshly ground black pepper

In a very large saucepan, mix the shallot and garlic with the oil. Cook over low heat, partially covered, stirring occasionally, until the onion is tender, about 10 minutes.

Add the tomatoes and cook, uncovered, over medium heat, until just heated through, about 1 to 2 minutes. Stir in the parsley and vinegar, and season with salt and pepper to taste.

KETCHUP

Although not as popular these days as salsa, ketchup is still one of the most versatile, and certainly the most American, of all sauces, even if the British do claim its origin as theirs.

Use as you would any ketchup.

Makes about 4 cups

5 pounds ripe Italian plum (Roma) tomatoes, cored and coarsely chopped

1 large yellow onion, coarsely chopped

1 large Granny Smith apple, cored, seeded, and coarsely chopped

1 celery rib, coarsely chopped

2 6-ounce cans tomato paste

¾ cup light brown sugar

1¼ cups red wine vinegar

8 whole cloves

½ teaspoon celery seed

2 tablespoons sweet Hungarian paprika

1 teaspoon cinnamon

2 teaspoons ancho or regular chili powder

½ teaspoon allspice

1 teaspoon fennel seed

½ teaspoon anise seed

1 teaspoon black peppercorns

1 tablespoon kosher salt

Mix all the ingredients in a large (nonaluminum) stockpot and bring to a boil, then reduce the heat and simmer, partially covered, for 1 hour. In a blender or food processor, purée until just smooth, then press through a fine strainer and discard any fibrous material in the strainer.

Return to the pot and simmer, stirring frequently, until the ketchup is thick but still pourable, about 1½ hours. Taste, and add a little more vinegar, brown sugar, or salt if necessary.

Ladle 1 cup ketchup into a jar and refrigerate for current use. The rest can be placed in plastic freezer bags and frozen for up to 3 months.

MARINARA SAUCE

This is my all-purpose, year-round, always-some-in-the-freezer tomato sauce. It has a rich tomato flavor, is chunky but not too thick, with herb flavors. Sometimes, just before serving, I stir some shredded fresh basil leaves into the sauce.

Serve with pasta, on vegetables, or use in casseroles. It makes an excellent pizza sauce.

Makes about 10 cups

1 large onion, finely chopped

3 large garlic cloves, finely chopped

2 teaspoons olive oil

3 28-ounce cans chopped or crushed
    tomatoes in purée

2 12-ounce cans tomato vegetable juice

1 teaspoon crushed dried rosemary

2 teaspoons crushed dried marjoram

1 teaspoon crushed dried thyme

2 teaspoons crushed dried basil

In a large pot, mix together the onion, garlic, and oil. Cook over low heat for 15 minutes, stirring frequently, to tenderize the onion. Mix in the chopped or crushed tomatoes, vegetable juice, and crushed dried herbs, bring to a boil, then reduce the heat and simmer gently for 1 hour, stirring occasionally to prevent scorching.

For a smooth sauce, purée in a blender. Either refrigerate for up to 1 week or freeze for up to 3 months.

PUTTANESCA SAUCE

According to myth, this sauce was thrown together and then tossed over some pasta by the prostitutes of Rome when the police came banging at the door, thus allowing the women to claim their male companions were only "dinner guests." It's a wild, brash, coarse sauce, with a distinct flavor of capers, chock-full of the impudent flavors of central Italy.

Serve with roast pork or with store-bought pasta, such as penne, rotini, or rigatoni. The sauce also can be spread over pizza or onto focaccia dough.

Makes about 1½ cups

1 small onion, coarsely chopped

2 large garlic cloves, coarsely chopped

2 teaspoons extra-virgin or virgin olive oil

1 35-ounce can peeled Italian plum tomatoes, drained and coarsely chopped (optional)

¼ cup tomato paste

2 tablespoons balsamic vinegar

2 tablespoons capers

1 tablespoon pitted and coarsely chopped calamata olives

¼ teaspoon hot red pepper flakes

Salt and freshly ground black pepper

In a large saucepan, mix the onion and garlic with the oil and cook over low heat, partially covered, stirring occasionally, until the onion is tender, about 10 minutes. Do not brown.

Add the tomatoes, tomato paste, and vinegar, mix well, bring to a boil, then reduce the heat and simmer for 5 minutes, uncovered, stirring often. Stir in the capers, olives, and red pepper, if using. Simmer for another 8 to 10 minutes to form a thick, chunky sauce. Season with salt and black pepper to taste.

RAW TOMATO CONCASSÉE

This is the simplest and freshest of all possible tomato sauces—just peeled, seeded, diced tomatoes seasoned lightly with salt and pepper—so use only the finest, vine-ripened tomatoes.

Serve on warm pasta, pass alongside steamed or boiled fresh vegetables, spoon over cold poached, sautéed, or grilled fish.

Makes about 2 cups

> **2 pounds ripe plum or heirloom tomatoes**
> **Kosher or sea salt**
> **Freshly ground black pepper**

With a sharp paring knife, cut a shallow X into each tomato at the core end. Drop 4 or 5 tomatoes at a time into a large pot of simmering water and allow them to blanch for about 15 seconds. Immediately remove with a skimmer or slotted spoon, set aside, and repeat with the remaining tomatoes.

When tomatoes are cool enough to handle, use the tip of the paring knife to slip off the skins.

Cut each tomato in half, around its belly, and gently squeeze out the seeds. With a serrated knife, cut into small dice. If the tomatoes are watery, place in a strainer and allow to drain for 15 minutes. Otherwise, season with a little salt and pepper and serve.

FRESH ITALIAN RAGU

With its pale pink color and rich tomato flavor accented by the intense taste of tiny pieces of prosciutto, this Italian favorite is one of the great tomato sauces of the world.

Serve on pasta or steamed mixed vegetables, spoon over asparagus to make into an appetizer, or use on grilled fish, such as halibut or salmon fillets.

Makes about 3 cups

1 tablespoon onion, finely chopped
1 tablespoon carrot, finely chopped
2 tablespoons prosciutto, finely chopped
1 teaspoon olive oil
2 cups Raw Tomato Concassée (page 59)

¼ teaspoon fresh thyme, finely chopped
¼ teaspoon fresh rosemary, finely chopped
2 tablespoons heavy cream
Salt and freshly ground black pepper

Mix the onion, carrot, and prosciutto with the oil in a nonstick sauté pan and place over low heat. Partially cover and cook, stirring occasionally, until carrots are very tender, about 20 minutes. Add the Concassée, thyme, and rosemary and simmer gently until the mixture reaches a slightly thickened sauce consistency, about 10 to 15 minutes.

Add the cream and cook 1 minute longer. Taste, and season with a little salt and pepper if needed.

EXTRA-EASY SUNDRIED TOMATO SAUCE

This lightly textured sauce has a complex flavor since it is made with stock and V-8 juice.

Serve with broiled or grilled chicken, or pass alongside broiled or grilled steaks. Also excellent with roast leg of lamb, venison, or buffalo. If made with vegetable stock, the sauce is perfect on steamed or boiled vegetables.

Makes about 2 cups

12 sundried tomato halves
1 cup chicken, beef, or vegetable stock
½ cup V-8 juice
1 tablespoon sherry vinegar

1 teaspoon fresh cilantro, finely chopped
1 teaspoon fresh basil, finely chopped
1 teaspoon fresh parsley, finely chopped
Salt and freshly ground black pepper

Simmer the sundried tomatoes in the stock until very tender, about 6 to 8 minutes. Pour into a blender, add the V-8 juice, vinegar, and purée until very smooth. Add a little more juice, if necessary, to thin the sauce to a nice pouring consistency. Add herbs and season with salt and pepper to taste. Reheat in a small saucepan over medium heat. Serve hot.

Note: The recipe for chicken stock is on page 82; for beef stock, page 79; and for vegetable stock, page 85.

SUNDRIED TOMATO AND
DILL MUSTARD SAUCE

Although thickly textured, this mustard sauce has a light, fresh flavor.

Use as a condiment for roasted or grilled lamb, or pass alongside roast beef or steak. Serve with cold meats, like cold roast pork or beef, or use as a dipping sauce for boiled shrimp. This sauce is a good substitute for any spicy mustard, adding zip to hamburgers, or sausages, and sandwiches.

Makes 1¼ cups

24 sundried tomato halves, finely chopped
½ cup Dijon mustard
½ cup fresh dill, finely chopped
Freshly ground black pepper

Cover the tomatoes with the hottest possible tapwater and allow to soak until tender, about 5 minutes. Drain, and either pound in a mortar or smash with the back of a spoon in a bowl, to form a paste. Mix well with the mustard and dill. Season with pepper to taste. Refrigerate until serving time.

Sundried Tomato, Garlic, and Parsley Mustard Sauce

Substitute parsley for the dill and mix in 1 small garlic clove, finely chopped.

VIRGIN BLOODY MARY SAUCE

This mild Bloody Mary sauce has a big early morning garden bouquet and a tangy fresh vegetable flavor with a subtle horseradish aroma. For a hotter sauce, add a teaspoon or so of Hot Red Pepper Sauce (page 104) or a store-bought pepper sauce.

Serve as a dipping sauce with raw oysters, raw or fried clams, soft-shell crabs, or whole cooked shrimp. Extra sauce can be refrigerated and served as a drink, with or without vodka.

Makes about 2½ cups

1½ cups tomato vegetable juice

1 cup tomato juice

1 tablespoon red wine vinegar

½ teaspoon celery seed

2 tablespoons Worcestershire sauce

1 teaspoon prepared white horseradish
   (not a creamy horseradish sauce)

¼ teaspoon freshly ground black pepper

Put all the ingredients in a blender and whirl until well combined.

YELLOW PEPPER TOMATO SAUCE

With the sweet but somewhat brash flavor of the peppers tempered by the herb-flavored tomato sauce, this unexpectedly colorful winter sauce will enrich any lunch or dinner. To make the sauce in summer, substitute a fresh tomato sauce for the marinara.

Serve with poached or grilled fish, roasted or grilled chicken, or steamed vegetables. Use this sauce with store-bought, dried pasta; any small, textured pasta will do—such as penne or rigatoni, shells or fusilli, or cavatappi.

Makes about 4 cups

> 3 large yellow bell peppers, cored and
>   cut into strips about 1-inch long
> 2 cups Marinara Sauce (page 57) or
>   store-bought marinara sauce
> 2 tablespoons fresh parsley, finely chopped
> Freshly ground black pepper

Place the peppers in a very large microwave-safe bowl, cover tightly, and microwave on high (100 percent) for 8 minutes. Immediately uncover and stir in the marinara sauce and the parsley. Season lightly with the pepper.

5

......

SALAD DRESSINGS

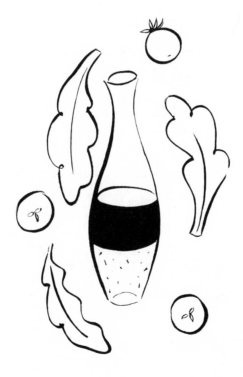

Creamy Avocado Lime Dressing

Beet and Raspberry Vinegar Dressing

Chickpea and Sherry Vinegar Dressing

Green Goddess Dressing

Honey Mustard Dressing with Balsamic Vinegar

Miso Lemon Dressing

Russian Dressing

Tartar Sauce

Thousand Island Dressing

CREAMY AVOCADO LIME DRESSING

This pale green, rosemary-scented dressing is smooth and creamy.

Serve with salads made of hearty greens, like romaine or escarole or spinach, with tomatoes or sliced red onions or grated carrots.

Makes about 1¼ cups

½ small, ripe avocado, seeded, peeled,
  and cut into 4 or 5 pieces
Juice of 1 lime
¾ cup skim milk
¼ teaspoon crushed dried rosemary
Salt and freshly ground black pepper

Whirl first 4 ingredients in a blender until smooth. Season with salt and pepper to taste. Store in a tightly covered jar in the refrigerator.

BEET AND RASPBERRY
VINEGAR DRESSING

This deep purple-red dressing has a fruity, full-bodied, slightly sweet flavor.

It is an elegant dressing for special occasions and is especially good served with mesclun (mixed baby lettuces) salads or as a sauce for cooked vegetable salads. Remember, though, that the dressing turns light-colored vegetables fuchsia!

If you have a juice extractor at home and want to make your own beet juice, you need to extract 2 large beets for this recipe.

Makes about 1 cup

¾ cup beet juice, available at juice bars in
    health- and whole-foods markets
2 tablespoons raspberry vinegar
Salt and freshly ground black pepper

Stir together the beet juice and vinegar. Season with salt and pepper to taste. If made ahead, store in a tightly covered jar in the refrigerator.

CHICKPEA AND SHERRY
VINEGAR DRESSING

This pale golden dressing has hints of sherry and a light acid finish.
   Use with green salads made of sturdy lettuces, like romaine, and textured with croutons or tomatoes.
Makes about 1 cup

½ cup juice from 1 16-ounce can of chickpeas,
   plus ½ cup chickpeas
2 tablespoons sherry vinegar
Salt and freshly ground black pepper

Whirl the juice, chickpeas, and vinegar together in a blender until smooth. Season with salt and pepper to taste. If made ahead, store in a tightly covered jar in the refrigerator.

GREEN GODDESS DRESSING

Created by the Palace Hotel in San Francisco, this pistachio-green sauce is colored by an abundance of fresh leaves and herbs.

Serve with green salads; use as a dressing for chicken, or fish salads; or as a dip with hors d'oeuvres.
Makes about 2½ cups

1 cup nonfat or lowfat buttermilk
½ cup fresh parsley leaves
½ cup fresh spinach leaves
½ cup watercress leaves
2 tablespoons fresh tarragon leaves

2 scallions, trimmed and cut into 4 to
    5 pieces
½ cup light sour cream
2 teaspoons tarragon vinegar
Salt and freshly ground black pepper

In a food processor, combine the buttermilk, parsley, spinach, watercress, tarragon, and scallions and purée until a bright green sauce forms and only the tiniest specks of green can be seen in the sauce, about 90 seconds. Whisk into the sour cream and vinegar and season with salt and pepper to taste.

Honey Mustard Dressing with Balsamic Vinegar

This popular mix of flavors will become a household favorite.

Use it to dress everyday salads tossed together just before dinner, or with seafood, chicken, or vegetable salads.

Makes about 1 cup

¼ cup Dijon mustard
2 tablespoons honey
1½ tablespoons balsamic vinegar
½ cup vegetable or chicken stock
Salt and freshly ground black pepper

In a bowl, whisk together the mustard and honey. Whisk in the vinegar, then gradually whisk in the stock. Season with salt and pepper to taste. Store in a tightly covered jar in the refrigerator.

Note: The recipe for vegetable stock is on page 85, and for chicken stock, page 82.

MISO LEMON DRESSING

Here is a very light, gently textured dressing with a hint of nutty, grain flavor from the miso and a refreshing zing from the lemon and pepper.

Use it to dress green salads of all kinds, from mesclun (mixed baby lettuces) to crisp iceberg and tomato salads.

Makes about ¾ cup

> ¼ cup yellow (barley) miso (available in Asian
>   markets and whole-foods markets)
> ½ cup chicken, beef, or vegetable stock
> Juice of ½ lemon
> Freshly ground black pepper

Measure the miso into a large bowl, then whisk in the stock and lemon juice. Season generously with pepper. Store in a tightly covered jar in the refrigerator.

RUSSIAN DRESSING

This audaciously flavored dressing was originally made with caviar, which is why it's named "Russian." Now we use chopped bell peppers and celery.

I can't imagine an iceberg lettuce salad without this dressing, but it can also be used on crab, shrimp, oyster, or chicken salads. As a spread, use on chicken, turkey, ham, or roast beef sandwiches.

Makes about 1¾ cups

1 cup light sour cream
½ cup store-bought chili sauce or
  Cocktail Sauce (page 54)
2 tablespoons green bell pepper, finely
  chopped
2 tablespoons red bell pepper, finely
  chopped

2 tablespoons celery, finely
  chopped
2 teaspoons Worcestershire sauce
Juice of ¼ large lemon
Salt and freshly ground black
  pepper

Stir together the sour cream, chili sauce or Cocktail Sauce, green pepper, red pepper, celery, Worcestershire, and lemon juice. Season with salt and pepper to taste. Store in a tightly covered jar in the refrigerator.

TARTAR SAUCE

This is a full-flavored, lowfat version of the classic sauce often served with fried fish.
  Serve with hot or cold fish, or use on sandwiches.
Makes about 1¼ cups

1 cup light sour cream
2 tablespoons low- or nonfat buttermilk
1 tablespoon dill pickle, finely chopped
Juice of ¼ lemon
2 teaspoons Dijon mustard

1 tablespoon parsley, finely chopped
1 tablespoon scallions, white part only,
  finely chopped
Salt and freshly ground black pepper

Stir together the sour cream, buttermilk, pickle, lemon juice, mustard, parsley, and scallions. Season with salt and pepper to taste. Store in a tightly covered jar in the refrigerator.

THOUSAND ISLAND DRESSING

This lightly textured, rust-colored sauce is a lowfat version of the classic.
  Serve as a spread on fish sandwiches, or use as a dressing for crisp green-leaved salads.
Makes about 1 ¼ cups

½ cup light sour cream
½ cup low- or nonfat buttermilk
1 tablespoon scallions, white part only, finely chopped
3 tablespoons store-bought chili sauce or Cocktail Sauce (page 54)

1 hard-boiled egg, white only, finely chopped
1 tablespoon fresh tarragon, finely chopped, or 1 teaspoon crushed dried tarragon
Salt and freshly ground black pepper

Stir together the sour cream, buttermilk, scallions, chili sauce or Cocktail Sauce, and egg white. Season with salt and pepper to taste. Store in a tightly covered jar in the refrigerator.

6

......

MEAT, FISH, AND POULTRY STOCKS AND FLAVORED SAUCES

In today's lighter and healthier home cooking, there is considerably less reliance on these classically oriented meat-, fish-, and poultry-flavored stocks and sauces that take long hours to prepare. Yet occasionally, there is still a need for them. Although there are no shortcuts to preparing a fine brown beef stock, here is a simple and easy-to-prepare microwave version of chicken stock and a brown fish sauce that can be made in just a few minutes.

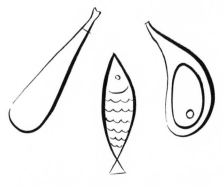

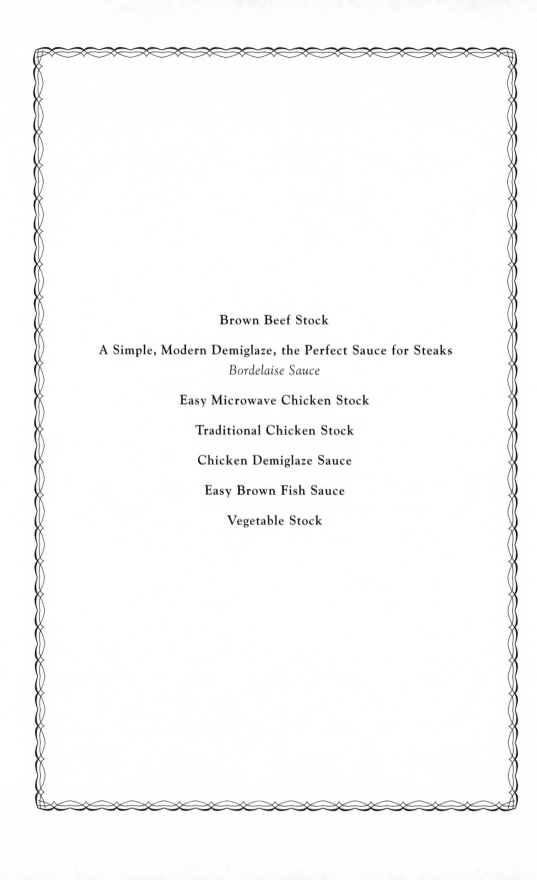

Brown Beef Stock

A Simple, Modern Demiglaze, the Perfect Sauce for Steaks
Bordelaise Sauce

Easy Microwave Chicken Stock

Traditional Chicken Stock

Chicken Demiglaze Sauce

Easy Brown Fish Sauce

Vegetable Stock

BROWN BEEF STOCK

Makes 4 quarts

4 pounds beef chuck, trimmed of fat and cut into 4 or 5 pieces

3 pounds beef bones, sawed into 1-inch pieces

2 to 3 pounds veal knuckle bones, sawed into 1-inch pieces

1 quart hottest tapwater

5 quarts cold tapwater

2 medium onions, trimmed, peeled, and halved

3 celery stalks, washed and cut into 3 or 4 pieces each

3 carrots, trimmed, scrubbed, and cut into 3 or 4 pieces each

3 large leeks, white parts only, cut into 1-inch pieces and thoroughly rinsed

6 garlic cloves, unpeeled

2 teaspoons dried thyme

2 teaspoons dried rosemary

4 bay leaves, crumbled

2 teaspoons black peppercorns

Roast the meat and bones at 375°F until well browned but not burned, about 2 hours, turning 2 or 3 times to ensure even coloring.

Transfer the meat and bones to a large stockpot. Pour the fat out of the roasting pan and place the pan across 2 burners set on high heat. Add 1 quart of hot water to the pan and scrape the bottom so that all the brown bits mix into the water as it comes to a boil. Carefully pour into the stockpot and add the cold water. Bring to just about the boiling point, then reduce the heat and simmer, partially covered, for 3 to 4 hours. Skim off all the fat and any scum that has risen to the top of the stock.

Add the vegetables, herbs, and peppercorns, and simmer for 16 more hours, skimming occasionally. Ladle the stock though a large strainer lined with cheesecloth and chill. Stock can be stored overnight in the refrigerator or frozen for up to 3 months.

A Simple, Modern Demiglaze, the Perfect Sauce for Steaks

This is the simplest—and many chefs would argue the best—sauce for a grilled steak. It has an intense beef flavor, a gelatinous texture that gently coats, and a depth of color and aroma that enhances all the best qualities of a great steak. For an even more complex sauce, prepare the red wine and shallot (Bordelaise Sauce) variation.

The real limitation of this sauce for the home cook is that it requires homemade beef stock. If you are not planning to make your own, you might try asking the chef at a restaurant you frequent if s/he would sell you a couple of quarts of beef stock.

Makes about 1 cup

**2 quarts homemade or store-bought
"house-made" brown beef stock**

Pour the stock through a cheesecloth-lined strainer into a large saucepan. Bring to a gentle boil over medium-high heat and allow to reduce slowly, never at a rapid boil, until a dark sauce forms that has a texture a little thicker than heavy cream, about 1 hour.

This sauce can be refrigerated for 2 to 3 days (just reheat when needed) or frozen for up to 3 months.

Bordelaise Sauce

When the Demiglaze has reduced to about 3 cups, add 1 cup full-bodied red wine, 1 finely chopped shallot, a small pinch of dried thyme, and 1 bay leaf to the stock and continue reducing until the sauce reaches the proper consistency. Strain and season with a little salt if necessary.

Easy Microwave Chicken Stock

Making chicken stock in the microwave is easier and quicker than making it conventionally. All you do is combine the ingredients, cover, and microwave them for 45 minutes. The result is as good as, if not better than, traditionally made stock.

Makes about 6 cups

2 large whole chicken breasts, bone-in, skin and fat removed, cut into 5 to 6 pieces
1 medium onion, trimmed and peeled
½ celery rib, leaves removed
1 small carrot, trimmed and scrubbed

2 garlic cloves, unpeeled
1 bay leaf
Small pinch of dried thyme
Big pinch of salt
7 cups cold tapwater

Place all the ingredients in a very large microwave-safe bowl. Seal with a double layer of plastic wrap, slip a soup plate under the bowl to catch any stock that seeps under the plastic film, and microwave on high (100 percent) for 45 minutes.

Carefully ladle the stock through a strainer lined with cheesecloth or a dampened towel. Stock can be stored overnight in the refrigerator or frozen for up to 3 months.

TRADITIONAL CHICKEN STOCK

Makes about 4 quarts

5 pounds raw chicken, meat and bones, without skin

5 quarts cold tapwater

2 celery ribs, washed and cut into 2- to 3-inch lengths

2 medium carrots, trimmed, scrubbed, and cut into 2- to 3-inch lengths

1 medium onion, trimmed, peeled, and quartered

½ turnip, thickly peeled, and quartered

1½ large leeks, white parts only, washed thoroughly

1 large tomato, cored and cut in half

1 large garlic clove, peeled

1 teaspoon dried thyme

½ teaspoon dried rosemary

3 parsley sprigs

½ teaspoon black peppercorns

2 whole cloves

1 crumbled bay leaf

In a large soup kettle or stockpot, combine the chicken and bones, and water. There should be enough water to cover all the ingredients by just about an inch. If not, add more water.

Bring to a simmer (*not a boil*) over medium heat and simmer, partially covered, for 2½ to 3 hours. Occasionally, skim the stock to remove the fat, foam, and sediment that have risen to the surface. Add the remaining ingredients and simmer for 1 hour longer.

Ladle the stock through a strainer lined with cheesecloth or a dampened towel. Stock can be stored overnight in the refrigerator or frozen for up to 3 months.

CHICKEN DEMIGLAZE SAUCE

Like its counterpart in the beef world, this is called a demiglaze in French terminology. It has a natural intensity, a depth of color, and a fine, full aroma.

Serve with roasted, broiled, grilled, sautéed, or poached chicken or game birds.

Makes about 1 cup

> **2 quarts Easy Microwave Chicken Stock
> (page 81) or Traditional Chicken Stock
> (page 82)**

Pour the stock through a cheesecloth-lined strainer into a large saucepan. Bring to a gentle boil over medium-high heat and allow to reduce slowly, never at a rapid boil, until a dark sauce forms that has a texture a little thicker than heavy cream, about 1 hour.

This sauce can be refrigerated for 2 to 3 days (just reheat when needed) or frozen for up to 3 months.

White Wine Chicken Demiglaze Sauce

When the Demiglaze has reduced to about 3 cups, add 1 cup dry white wine and continue reducing until the sauce reaches the proper consistency.

EASY BROWN FISH SAUCE

This light, brothlike sauce has a chestnut brown color with a rich, pleasant fish flavor and aroma.

Serve under poached or grilled salmon, tuna, or swordfish; or with poached or baked monkfish or halibut. Use as a dipping sauce for boiled shrimp.

Makes 2 cups

½ cup Chinese oyster sauce (available in most
   supermarkets and Asian groceries)
1½ cups chicken or vegetable stock
Big pinch of freshly ground black pepper

Stir all the ingredients together in a saucepan and bring to a boil. Serve at once.

VEGETABLE STOCK

Makes about 2 quarts

3 medium carrots, trimmed, scrubbed, and cut into 5 or 6 pieces each

4 large leeks, white parts only, split lengthwise, thoroughly washed to remove all grit, and cut into 3 or 4 pieces each

3 large shallots, peeled

2 medium onions, trimmed, peeled, and quartered

3 celery ribs, washed and cut into 4 or 5 pieces each

1 pound zucchini, trimmed, washed, and cut into 1-inch lengths

2 large tomatoes, washed, cored, and quartered

1 large sweet red bell pepper, washed, cored, and cut into 6 or 8 pieces

1 medium turnip, trimmed, peeled, and cut into 6 or 8 pieces

1 medium parsnip, trimmed, peeled thickly, and cut into 6 or 8 pieces

2 garlic cloves, peeled

½-inch piece fresh gingerroot, peeled and cut in half lengthwise

3 sprigs fresh parsley

2 bay leaves

2 quarts cold tapwater

1 teaspoon black peppercorns

Pinch of salt

In a food processor, finely chop everything except water, peppercorns, and salt. Transfer to a large pot. Add the water and peppercorns and bring almost to a boil over medium heat. Reduce the heat and simmer, partially covered, for 2 hours.

Carefully ladle the stock through a strainer lined with cheesecloth, pressing firmly on the vegetables so they release all their liquid. Discard the vegetables. Stock can be stored overnight in the refrigerator or frozen for up to 3 months.

7

......

Yogurt and
Sour Cream Sauces

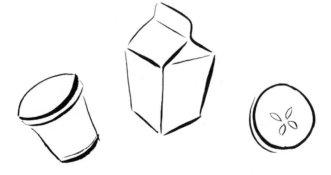

Lightly Minted Cucumber Sauce

My Grandmother's Fresh Dill and Mint Sauce

Emerald Green Sauce

Fresh Horseradish
Pink Horseradish

Horseradish Cream Sauce
Herbed Horseradish Cream Sauce

Light Sour Cream "Mayonnaise"

Two-Mustard Sauce

Miso Saffron Sauce

LIGHTLY MINTED CUCUMBER SAUCE

Taking its cue from the icy raitas of Indian cooking, this sauce of refreshing shreds of cucumber is enlivened with fresh mint and lime.

Serve with smoked fish, like sturgeon or mackerel, or alongside a fiery stew of beef or lamb, or with lighter-flavored fish like flounder or sole. It is delicious on cold poached, broiled, or grilled chicken.

Makes about 2 cups

1 cup nonfat plain (unflavored) yogurt
1 large cucumber, peeled, seeded, and finely grated
1 tablespoon fresh mint, finely chopped
Juice of ½ small lime
Salt and freshly ground black pepper

Stir together the yogurt, cucumber, mint, and lime juice. Season with salt and pepper to taste. Refrigerate until serving time.

MY GRANDMOTHER'S FRESH DILL
AND MINT SAUCE

This is a thick, gorgeous green sauce vibrantly alive with the fresh flavors of dill and mint.

Use as a dressing for chopped summer vegetables, or for chicken or shrimp salads. Makes a tasty spread for sliced turkey or chicken, or roast beef sandwiches. Dollop it on cold grilled meats, from chicken breasts to lamb chops.

Makes about 1¼ cups

> **1 cup light sour cream**
> **½ cup fresh dill, finely chopped**
> **¼ cup fresh mint, finely chopped**
> **Salt and freshly ground black pepper**

Stir together the sour cream, dill, and mint. Season with salt and pepper to taste. Refrigerate until serving time.

EMERALD GREEN SAUCE

This incredibly fresh tasting, speckled green sauce has all the big, complex flavors of the most popular herbs: parsley, cilantro, dill, and tarragon.

Spoon over hot or cold cooked vegetables to make an extraordinary vegetarian dish; use as a sauce for richly flavored fish like salmon or swordfish; or serve with a roasted leg of lamb instead of mint jelly. As a dressing, use with vegetable or fish salads; as a dip, this sauce is excellent with raw or cooked vegetables.

Makes 2½ cups

½ cup tightly packed parsley leaves
½ cup tightly packed cilantro leaves
½ cup tightly packed dill leaves
½ cup tightly packed tarragon leaves

Juice of ½ small lime
1 cup nonfat yogurt or light sour cream
Salt and freshly ground black pepper

In a food processor, purée the parsley, cilantro, dill, tarragon, lime, and yogurt or sour cream until a smooth sauce forms, about 90 seconds. Season with salt and pepper to taste.

FRESH HORSERADISH

Homemade horseradish has about 5 times the intensity of the store-bought variety. Even so, when made fresh, with a fine vinegar, it will have unexpected subtleties in flavor.

Use, if a bit sparingly, anytime a recipe calls for horseradish; or serve a small spoonful alongside richly smoked fish, like mackerel.

Makes about 1½ cups

> **1 pound fresh horseradish root, ends trimmed**
>   **and peeled**
> **½ cup sherry or champagne vinegar**

In a food processor, either finely grate or process the horseradish with the metal blade to form a very fine meal. Add the vinegar and mix well.

Store in tightly covered glass jar in the refrigerator for up to 3 months.

Pink Horseradish

Grate 1 small, peeled beet with the horseradish.

HORSERADISH CREAM SAUCE

Similar to the English horseradish cream sauce served with roast beef, this light version is thicker in texture and has unexpected hints of garlic.

Serve with roast beef or leg of lamb, or with very rich seafood, like swordfish, salmon, sturgeon, or tuna. Use as a topping for baked potatoes, steamed or boiled winter root vegetables.

Makes about 1 cup

> 1-cup container reduced-fat sour cream
> 1½ tablespoons Fresh Horseradish (page 92)
> 1 small garlic clove, peeled and finely chopped
> Salt and freshly ground black pepper

Whisk together the sour cream, fresh horseradish, and garlic. Season with salt and pepper to taste. Refrigerate until serving time.

Herbed Horseradish Cream Sauce

Whisk 1 heaping tablespoon of finely chopped fresh herbs into the sauce. Use dill when serving with strongly flavored fish like salmon, tuna, and swordfish; use tarragon with chicken; parsley with beef; rosemary or mint with lamb.

LIGHT SOUR CREAM "MAYONNAISE"

This simple sauce of light sour cream flavored with mustard and lemon juice takes only seconds to prepare and is decidedly reminiscent of mayonnaise.

Use as a substitute for mayonnaise in a dressing or spread, or serve as a light sauce on poached chicken or lighter-flavored fish, like sole or halibut. Also excellent as a dip or sauce to accompany raw or cooked vegetables, or as a dressing for chicken, fish, or vegetable salads.

Makes about 1¼ cups

1 cup light sour cream
3 tablespoons Dijon mustard
2 teaspoons freshly squeezed lemon juice
Salt and freshly ground black pepper

Whisk together the sour cream, mustard, and lemon juice. Season with salt and pepper to taste. Refrigerate until serving time.

Two-Mustard Sauce

This spreadlike sauce has obvious but not overpowering mustardy textures. It can be used as with any mustard, but it's a lighter, more interesting condiment than the usual variety.

Use as a dip for raw or cooked vegetables, to accompany sautéed, broiled, or grilled fish, or pass with grilled chicken breasts. Spread on ham or roast beef sandwiches, or dollop a heaping tablespoon into a richly textured soup like minestrone or a cold soup like borscht.

Makes 1¼ cups

> 2 tablespoons Düsseldorf, Creole, or Dijon mustard
> 2 tablespoons coarsely cracked mustard
> ½ cup nonfat plain yogurt
> ½ cup light sour cream
> Salt and freshly ground black pepper

Stir together the mustard, yogurt, and sour cream. Season with salt and pepper to taste. Refrigerate until serving time.

MISO SAFFRON SAUCE

This thick, light gold sauce has an intense flavor with hints of saffron and lemon.

Serve as a dip with chips, as a cold sauce to accompany sliced cold roast pork or beef, or as a dressing for cold salads made with seafood. Spread on fish sandwiches like Louisiana's famous Poor Boy.
Makes 1¼ cups

1 cup light sour cream
3 tablespoons white miso
½ teaspoon crushed saffron threads
Juice of ½ lemon
Salt and freshly ground black pepper

Stir together the sour cream, miso, saffron, and lemon juice. Season with salt and pepper to taste. Refrigerate until serving time.

8

......

BBQ AND CHILI SAUCES

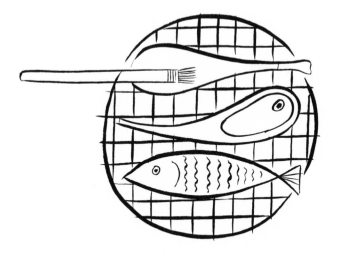

Basil Barbecue Sauce

Homemade Chili Powder
Fiery-Hot Chili Powder

Southwestern-Style Dried Chili Sauce
Easy Mole-Style Sauce

Jamaican Jerk Barbecue and Basting Sauce

Midwestern Barbecue Sauce

Hot Red Pepper Sauce

Hot Green Pepper Sauce

Hot Yellow Pepper Sauce with Saffron

Rouille

Texas Barbecue Sauce

BASIL BARBECUE SAUCE

This is one of my all-time favorite barbecue sauces. With its medium-thick texture and dark rust color, it is somewhat sweet and mildly chilied. It is enriched by a small handful of fresh basil added at the end of the cooking.

Serve alongside grilled or broiled chicken, beef, or lamb. Use as a marinade and basting sauce for grilled steak and chops. Perks up leftovers, like sliced, roasted meats or turkey; substitutes for store-bought ketchup on sandwiches or cold meats.

Makes about 4 cups

1 small yellow onion, finely chopped
2 large garlic cloves, finely chopped
1-inch piece fresh gingerroot, peeled and
   finely chopped
1 teaspoon olive or canola oil
1 cup tomato sauce
1 cup ketchup
1 cup dry red wine

2 tablespoons balsamic vinegar
2 tablespoons Worcestershire sauce
2 tablespoons soy sauce
2 tablespoons light brown sugar
2 tablespoons chili powder
1 tablespoon crushed dried basil
Salt and freshly ground black pepper
½ cup fresh basil leaves

In a large saucepan, mix the onion, garlic, and ginger with the oil. Sauté over medium heat until wilted, about 4 minutes. Stir in the tomato sauce, ketchup, red wine, vinegar, Worcestershire sauce, soy sauce, sugar, chili powder, and dried basil. Bring to a boil, reduce the heat, and simmer for 30 minutes. Season with salt and pepper to taste.

In small batches, puree the sauce in a blender, holding a thick towel securely over the blender jar to prevent the sauce from spewing all over the kitchen. Add the basil leaves to the last batch and blend for just a few seconds to chop and distribute the basil through the sauce.

Can be refrigerated, tightly covered, for 2 to 3 days or frozen for up to 3 months. Reheat, if necessary, before serving.

HOMEMADE CHILI POWDER

Much better than store-bought, this is a full-flavored, hot but not fiery chili powder. A fiery-hot varia-tion follows.

Ancho chili powder is sold in some supermarkets and most Hispanic markets. Generally, it is finely granulated, rather than powdered, so grind it to a fine powder in a spice mill before using to prevent the sauce from having a gritty texture.

Makes about ¾ cup

½ cup ancho chili powder (2 ounces
    by weight)
2 tablespoons Hungarian sweet paprika
1 tablespoon ground cumin
1 teaspoon crushed dried thyme
1 teaspoon crushed dried oregano
1 teaspoon crushed dried rosemary

1 teaspoon garlic powder
1 teaspoon onion powder
½ teaspoon ground cardamom
½ teaspoon ground coriander
¼ teaspoon ground cinnamon
⅛ teaspoon white pepper
⅛ teaspoon freshly ground black pepper

Mix together all the ingredients until well blended. Sift through a fine strainer to remove any hard, ground-up pieces from the pods of the various spices. Can be stored, tightly covered, in a cool kitchen cabinet for up to 6 months.

Fiery-Hot Chili Powder

Substitute hot Hungarian paprika for the sweet, add ¼ teaspoon ground cayenne pepper, and increase both the black pepper and the white pepper to ¼ teaspoon each.

SOUTHWESTERN-STYLE DRIED CHILI SAUCE

This thick sauce uses two different chilies to give it a breadth of chili flavors. Follow the precautions on page xiv for seeding hot peppers.

Use as a condiment, like ketchup, to spice up other sauces or dips; or add to pan dripping to form a spicy gravy. Serve with roasted or braised meats, like chicken, pork, lamb, or beef. Also good as a glaze and sauce for baked, roasted, or grilled fish.

Make about 2 cups

2 ounces (2 medium) dried ancho chilies
2 ounces (about 10 medium) dried guajillo chilies
10 dried tomato halves
2½ cups water or any of the stock recipes on
   pages 79, 81, 82, 85
1 tablespoon balsamic vinegar

Wearing plastic gloves, tear the chilies open, remove and discard all the seeds and ribs. To soften the chilies, either place the chilies and tomatoes in a microwave-safe bowl, add the water or stock, and microwave on high (100 percent) for 7 minutes; or place the chilies and tomatoes in a large bowl, bring the water or stock to a boil, and then pour it over the dried chilies and tomatoes and set the bowl aside for 1 hour.

Carefully pour the chilies and liquid into a blender, add the vinegar, cover, and holding the cover securely in place with a thick towel, blend until a thick, smooth sauce forms.

Easy Mole-Style Sauce

Stir 1 heaping tablespoon unsweetened cocoa into 1 cup very hot, strong coffee. Substitute this cocoa-coffee for 1 cup of the water or broth in the recipe above.

JAMAICAN JERK BARBECUE AND BASTING SAUCE

This thick, onion-flavored barbecue sauce is generously spiced with allspice, which is indigenous to Jamaica. In its orthodox version, the sauce would be scaldingly hot, calling for about 10 Scotch bonnets, the hottest of all peppers. Here the sauce has been cooled down—though it is still somewhat hot—to ½ Scotch bonnet or 1 whole large jalapeño.

Use as a marinade and barbecue sauce for fish that is to be baked or broiled, or for grilled, baked or broiled chicken, beef, or pork. This is an excellent sandwich spread as well.

Makes about 2 cups

½ Scotch bonnet pepper, cored and seeded (or 1 large jalapeño)

5 thin scallions, trimmed and cut into 4 or 5 pieces each

1 small red onion, quartered

1 large shallot, quartered

2-inch piece fresh gingerroot, peeled and quartered

4 large garlic cloves

1 tablespoon canola oil

¼ cup soy sauce

Juice of 1 lime

Juice of 1 lemon

Juice of 1 orange

1 tablespoon dried thyme

1 tablespoon ground allspice

1 teaspoon each ground cinnamon, coriander, and cardamom

½ teaspoon ground cloves

½ teaspoon freshly ground black pepper

½ teaspoon ground white pepper

1 tablespoon light brown sugar

1 teaspoon salt

In a food processor, process the pepper, scallions, onion, shallot, ginger, garlic, and oil until everything is well chopped. Add the remaining ingredients and process until the mixture is well blended, about 60 seconds.

Use immediately or store in a tightly covered jar in the refrigerator for up to 1 week.

MIDWESTERN BARBECUE SAUCE

This is a top-notch, lightly sweetened, spicy and hot midwestern-style barbecue sauce with a spectacular aroma and the color of antique-finished mahogany.

Serve with beef, pork, lamb, chicken, or turkey, or spread on sandwiches. This sauce can also be used for glazing roasts, or it can be brushed over grilled meats and fish during charcoal cooking. Use it as a key ingredient in barbecued beef, chicken, or pork.

Make about 2 cups

¾ cup Homemade Chili Powder (page 100)
1 cup ketchup
1¼ cups water
2 tablespoons honey

In a large saucepan, whisk all the ingredients together until a smooth, thick barbecue sauce forms. Bring to a boil over medium heat, stirring frequently, then reduce the heat and simmer for 5 minutes to dissolve the spices and allow the flavors to meld.

Refrigerate until needed. Leftover chili sauce can be frozen. Reheat, if necessary, before serving.

HOT RED PEPPER SAUCE

With a cleaner, hotter, more interesting flavor than commercial brands, this sauce is worth the few min-utes it takes for you to make it. Follow the precautions on page xiv for seeding hot peppers.

Serve anytime you would use store-bought hot red pepper sauce like Tabasco, using a few drops to 1 or 2 teaspoons, depending on your recipe.

Makes about ⅓ cup

4 ounces hot red peppers, preferably a combination of 2 or 3 different varieties, such as red finger peppers, jalapeños, habaneros, or the like

Juice of ½ lemon
1 teaspoon kosher salt
¼ cup water

Wearing plastic gloves to protect yourself, trim, seed, and core the peppers. In a food processor, combine the peppers with the lemon juice, salt, and water and process until a thin bright red liquid forms, about 2 minutes. Carefully pour into a fine strainer and press firmly on the pulp to extract the liquid.

Can be stored in a glass jar in the refrigerator for up to 1 month.

HOT GREEN PEPPER SAUCE

This green sauce is a little sweeter and slightly less hot than homemade Hot Red Pepper Sauce (page 104). Follow the precautions on page xiv for seeding hot peppers.

Shake a few drops into stews and casseroles made with vegetables, chicken, or beef, into Bloody Marys, or into green salsas.

Makes about ½ cup

½ small green bell pepper, stemmed, cored, seeded, and cut into chunks

4 ounces hot green peppers, preferably a combination of 2 or 3 different varieties, such as serrano and jalapeño

Juice of ½ lemon

1 teaspoon crushed dried rosemary

1 teaspoon crushed dried tarragon

½ teaspoon crushed dried thyme

1 teaspoon kosher salt

¼ cup water

Wearing plastic gloves to protect yourself, trim, seed, and core the hot peppers. In a food processor, combine the peppers with the lemon juice, rosemary, tarragon, thyme, salt, and water and process until a thin green liquid forms, about 2 minutes. Carefully pour into a fine strainer and press firmly on the pulp to extract the liquid.

Can be stored in a glass jar in the refrigerator for up to 1 month.

HOT YELLOW PEPPER SAUCE
WITH SAFFRON

With a gentler and sweeter flavor that is still quite hot, this sauce will sear the palate of the hot sauce lover in a most pleasing way. Follow the precautions on page xiv for dealing with hot peppers.

Serve this sauce on everything from fish to French fries, or use it to heat up a curry or a fish stew. It is especially good in chicken and lighter-flavored vegetable recipes that call for hot pepper sauce.
Makes about ½ cup

½ small yellow or orange bell pepper, stemmed, cored, seeded, and cut in 4 chunks

4 ounces hot yellow peppers, preferably a combination of 2 or 3 different varieties, such as yellow hot peppers and yellow or orange habaneros

¼ teaspoon saffron threads

Juice of ½ lemon

1 teaspoon kosher salt

¼ cup water

Wearing plastic gloves to protect yourself, trim, seed, and core the hot peppers. In a food processor, combine the peppers, saffron, lemon juice, salt, and water and process until a thin bright yellow liquid forms, about 2 minutes. Carefully pour into a fine strainer and press firmly on the pulp to extract the liquid.

Can be stored in a glass jar in the refrigerator for up to 1 month.

ROUILLE

Named for its rusty color (rouille means "rust" in French), this is a thick, garlicky hot sauce that will knock you dead. It is traditionally added to fish stews like bouillabaisse, but it is astoundingly more useful than just that.

Use this sauce discreetly as a sandwich spread, or thin it with extra tomato juice and serve it as dip. It's a fiery accompaniment to roasted cold meats, like beef, pork, and lamb, as well as broiled, grilled, or roasted chicken or turkey. Stir a little into soups and stews to add some zip.

Makes ¾ cup

3 large garlic cloves
1 very small, fresh, hot pepper (such as
    jalapeño or serrano), split and seeded
½ slice soft white bread, crusts removed
1 teaspoon tomato paste

1 tablespoon olive oil
Juice of ¼ lemon
2 teaspoons hot Hungarian paprika
¼ teaspoon freshly ground black pepper
¼ cup tomato juice

Purée everything in a food processor until very smooth. Taste carefully and adjust the seasonings.

Refrigerate until needed.

TEXAS BARBECUE SAUCE

This is a hot, spicy Western-style barbecue sauce.

Serve with beef, pork, lamb, chicken, or turkey, or spread on sandwiches. This sauce can also be used for glazing roasts, or it can be brushed over grilled meats and fish during charcoal cooking.

Makes 4 cups

2 cups ketchup

2 cups chili sauce

2 cups dark beer

½ cup Worcestershire sauce

¼ cup smooth, spicy mustard (such as Dijon, Creole, or spicy brown)

¼ cup brown sugar

2 tablespoons chili powder

2 teaspoons dried oregano

2 teaspoons Hot Red Pepper Sauce (page 104) or a store-bought pepper sauce

In a medium-size saucepan, whisk together all the ingredients and simmer uncovered, stirring occasionally, for 15 minutes. Set aside to cool.

Refrigerate until needed. Leftover chili sauce can be frozen. Reheat, if necessary, before serving.

9

......

MARINADES AS SAUCES

All of the marinades in this chapter can also be used as light sauces, either to spoon over the foods that were marinated in them, or as dipping sauces.

For light flavors, marinate fish for 15 to 30 minutes and poultry and meats for 1 to 2 hours; for more intense flavors, marinate fish for 1 to 2 hours and poultry and meats for 4 hours to overnight (in the refrigerator).

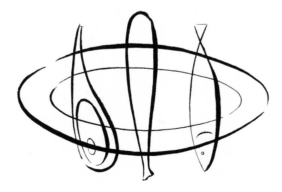

Anise-Flavored Marinade and Dipping Sauce

Honey Mustard Marinade and Dipping Sauce

Korean Marinade and Dipping Sauce

Laotian-Style Tamarind Marinade and Dipping Sauce

Moroccan-Style Marinade and Dipping Sauce

Sweet-and-Sour Transethnic Black Marinade and Dipping Sauce
Hot Sweet-and-Sour Black Sauce

Tandoori Marinade and Dipping Sauce

Teriyaki Marinade and Dipping Sauce

Tropp-Inspired Marinade and Dipping Sauce

Vietnamese Marinade and Dipping Sauce

ANISE-FLAVORED MARINADE AND DIPPING SAUCE

In this sweet sauce, the honey and anise slightly dominate all the other wonderful flavors—the ginger, the garlic, the shallots, and the rosemary.

Use as a marinade for large roasts of beef, lamb, or venison; or for strips of pork, lamb, or beef that are to be stir-fried or grilled. Use as a basting sauce for thick, meaty fish steaks that are to be broiled or grilled, or with lamb or veal chops. As a dipping sauce, serve with grilled meats and vegetables, steamed or boiled vegetables, or grilled fish fillets or steaks.

Makes about 2½ cups

3 shallots, peeled and quartered
4 garlic cloves
1½-inch piece fresh gingerroot, peeled
2 tablespoons dark sesame oil
Juice of 1 lemon
1 cup soy sauce

½ cup honey
¼ cup apple juice
2 bay leaves, crumbled
1 tablespoon crushed dried rosemary
1 tablespoon anise seed
1 teaspoon freshly ground black pepper

In a food processor, process the shallots, garlic, ginger, and oil until well chopped. Add the remaining ingredients and process until everything is well blended.

Refrigerate until needed (up to 2 weeks).

Honey Mustard Marinade and Dipping Sauce

This is a light marinade with garlic and herbs to support the honey and mustard flavors.

Use as a marinade with fish or chicken, as a dipping sauce with grilled or broiled fish or chicken breasts, or as an accompaniment to steamed, boiled, or raw vegetables or tofu.

Makes about 1¼ cups

¼ cup Dijon mustard

¼ cup coarsely cracked mustard

1 garlic clove, finely chopped

½ cup vegetable or chicken stock

½ teaspoon crushed dried tarragon

½ teaspoon crushed dried rosemary

Salt and freshly ground black pepper

Whisk together the mustards, garlic, stock, and herbs and allow the flavors to mellow for at least 1 hour before serving, then season with salt and pepper to taste.

Can be made up to 3 days ahead and refrigerated in a tightly covered container.

KOREAN MARINADE AND
DIPPING SAUCE

This dark brown, intensely flavored hot and sweet sauce is typical of Korean cooking.

Drizzle over hot or cold sliced roast beef or pork, serve alongside grilled or broiled steaks or lamb chops, or use as a marinade for game like buffalo and venison.

Makes about 1 cup

2 tablespoons dark sesame oil
⅓ cup brown sugar
⅓ cup soy sauce
2 garlic cloves, finely chopped
2 large shallots, finely chopped

1 tablespoon fresh gingerroot,
   finely chopped
½ teaspoon red pepper flakes
½ teaspoon freshly ground black pepper

Stir everything together and allow the flavors to mellow for about 30 minutes before serving as a sauce, or use immediately as a marinade.

Laotian-Style Tamarind Marinade and Dipping Sauce

This slightly sweet, slightly tart sauce is flavored with garlic, ginger, and anise. Tamarind paste, which is sold at Asian groceries and at premium supermarkets, gives this sauce its tartness and much of its dark color.

Serve with grilled or broiled salmon, tuna, or swordfish; or with pork chops or ham. Use as a marinade for beef or lamb roasts, for steak or lamb chops, or for broiled or grilled kabobs.

Makes about 1⅓ cups

2 small star anise, ground in a spice mill

3 garlic cloves, finely chopped

⅓ cup tamarind paste mixed with
  ½ cup water

2 teaspoons fresh gingerroot, grated

2 tablespoons soy sauce

1 teaspoon freshly ground black pepper

1 teaspoon brown sugar

1 teaspoon salt

2 tablespoons peanut oil

Stir everything together and allow the flavors to mellow for about 30 minutes before serving as a sauce, or use immediately as a marinade.

MOROCCAN-STYLE MARINADE AND DIPPING SAUCE

This brightly colored, slightly hot sauce is typical of the flavors of North Africa. For a less "hot" sauce, use sweet Hungarian paprika instead of the hot variety.

Serve as a sauce with roasted, poached, or broiled chicken or fish, especially the richer, darker-colored fish, like salmon, swordfish, and tuna. Use as a marinade for poultry or game, or for pork or lamb.
Makes about 1½ cups

½ cup cilantro, finely chopped
2 garlic cloves, finely chopped
2 tablespoons hot Hungarian paprika
2 teaspoons ground cumin
Juice of 1 lemon
½ cup stock

Stir everything together and allow the flavors to mellow for about 30 minutes before serving as a sauce, or use immediately as a marinade.

Sweet-and-Sour Transethnic Black Marinade and Dipping Sauce

This jet-black, intensely flavored sweet-and-sour sauce is made from balsamic vinegar (definitely Italian) and soy sauce (definitely not Italian) sweetened with brown sugar (if not exactly Caribbean, certainly from the Americas).

Use as a marinade for flank steak, strips of pork, beef, or lamb, or for large roasts of pork or beef; or for steaks or lamb chops that are to be grilled. As a light sauce, serve with broiled or grilled fish fillets and steaks.

Makes about 1¾ cups

1 cup balsamic vinegar
¼ cup soy sauce
½ cup brown sugar
1 garlic clove, coarsely chopped
½-inch piece fresh gingerroot, peeled and
    coarsely chopped

Whirl everything in a blender until the garlic and ginger have all but disintegrated, about 30 seconds. Allow to rest for 1 hour, then strain.

Hot Sweet-and-Sour Black Sauce

Add ½ of a small, fresh hot pepper, cored, seeded, and coarsely chopped, to the sauce before blending.

TANDOORI MARINADE AND DIPPING SAUCE

Although the list of spices in this mild curry sauce is extensive, the flavors are gentle and subtle.

Serve with raw or cooked vegetables as a dipping sauce; use as a sauce for cold cooked meats like lamb and beef; spread on sandwiches; or pass with roasted chicken or turkey. Use as a marinade for chicken or mildly flavored fish like halibut and mahimahi.

Makes 1½ cups

½ medium onion, finely chopped
6 garlic cloves, finely chopped
½-inch piece fresh gingerroot, peeled and
  grated
Juice of 1 lemon
1 cup plain nonfat yogurt
2 teaspoons ground coriander
2 teaspoons ground cardamom
1 teaspoon ground cumin
1 teaspoon ground turmeric

1 teaspoon garam masala (available in
  Asian groceries and premium markets)
¼ teaspoon mace
¼ teaspoon ground cloves
¼ teaspoon ground cinnamon
1 teaspoon salt
⅛ teaspoon white pepper
¼ teaspoon black pepper
⅛ teaspoon cayenne

Stir everything together and allow the flavors to mellow for about 30 minutes before serving as a sauce, or use immediately as a marinade.

Teriyaki Marinade and Dipping Sauce

Now an everyday standard, Teriyaki Sauce was once considered daring and exotic.
Use as a marinade for chicken, turkey, steak, or tofu or tempeh.
Makes about 1½ cups

1 cup soy sauce
2½-inch piece fresh gingerroot, peeled
  and coarsely chopped
2 large garlic cloves, coarsely chopped
½ teaspoon freshly ground black pepper

Juice of ½ lemon
Juice of ½ orange
2 tablespoons light brown sugar
2 teaspoons dark sesame oil

Whirl everything in a blender so that the flavors meld quickly and the garlic and ginger are so finely chopped as to almost disappear.

TROPP-INSPIRED MARINADE AND DIPPING SAUCE

This simple sauce, inspired by a recipe from Barbara Tropp, chef-owner of China Moon in San Francisco, is a perfect balance of typical Asian flavors—soy, shallot, ginger, and garlic—with an optional jalapeño for hotness.

Use as a marinade for poultry or game, or for steaks and chops; as a dipping sauce for fried vegetables, broiled or poached mildly flavored fish like sole, flounder, and halibut; or spoon a little under a poached, baked, or microwaved boneless chicken breast.

Makes about 1½ cups

1 cup soy sauce
2 tablespoons shallot, finely chopped
2 tablespoons fresh gingerroot, peeled and finely chopped
2 large garlic cloves, finely chopped
1 jalapeño, cored, seeded, and finely chopped (optional)
Freshly ground black pepper to taste

Stir everything together and allow the flavors to mellow for about 30 minutes before serving as a sauce, or use immediately as a marinade.

VIETNAMESE MARINADE AND DIPPING SAUCE

Here is a thin, light, ever so slightly fishy, somewhat salty sauce. It is boldly flavored with garlic and lime, with a hint of nuttiness from the sesame oil.

Lightly toss this sauce with steamed or boiled vegetables; add to stir-fries just before the end of their cooking time to heighten their flavors; or spoon under poached, broiled, or baked, mildly flavored fish like sole, flounder, and halibut.

Makes about 1 cup

½ cup nam pla (Vietnamese fish sauce, available at Asian groceries)

3 tablespoons fresh garlic, finely chopped

¼ cup lime juice

2 tablespoons sugar

2 teaspoons sesame oil

⅛ teaspoon cayenne

Stir everything together and allow the flavors to mellow for about 30 minutes before serving as a sauce, or use immediately as a marinade.

10

......

DESSERT SAUCES

Fresh Pineapple Orange Spice Sauce

Fresh Damson Plum Sauce

Fresh Star Fruit and Honey Sauce

Fresh Raspberry Purée
Fresh Strawberry Purée
Fresh Blackberry Purée, Fresh Blueberry Purée, or Fresh Mulberry Purée
Mango Pineapple Purée

Dried Cherry Sauce
Dried Blueberry Sauce, Dried Cranberry Sauce, Dried Banana Sauce,
or Dried Star Fruit Sauce
Dried Mission Fig Sauce or Dried Italian Plum Sauce

Strawberry Essence
Raspberry Essence, Blueberry Essence, or Dark Cherry Essence
Three-Berry Essence

Honey Lemon Sauce
Maple Syrup Sauce

Red Wine Dessert Sauce

FRESH PINEAPPLE ORANGE
SPICE SAUCE

This gently textured, golden sauce has a blend of pineapple and orange flavors accented with hints of spice.

Serve with fresh or poached fruits or berries, as a topping for light cakes, or at breakfast with pancakes or French toast.

Makes about 3 ½ cups

1 medium-size ripe pineapple, peeled,
  cored, and cut into 2-inch chunks
1 cup orange juice
¼ cup sugar

¼ teaspoon ground ginger
⅛ teaspoon ground cinnamon
⅛ teaspoon ground allspice
⅛ teaspoon ground coriander

In a food processor, thoroughly purée the pineapple. Transfer to a large saucepan, add the remaining ingredients, and bring to a boil over medium heat. Reduce the heat and simmer for 5 minutes to allow the flavors to blend. Serve hot, or refrigerate in a covered jar and serve cold.

FRESH DAMSON PLUM SAUCE

Damsons are small, blueberry-colored plums that make a late summer appearance at premium markets. They need only a few minutes of simmering to become a deep Beaujolais–colored sauce.

Serve with roast pork, venison, duck, or goose, or use cold as a dessert fruit sauce. Also delicious with pancakes, waffles, and French toast.

Makes about 2 cups

½ **cup hottest tapwater**
1 **cup sugar**
1 **quart fresh damson plums, stems**
    removed, any damaged plums discarded,
    and rinsed under cold running water
Juice of 1 lemon

Begin by softening the plums, either in the microwave or traditionally: in a large microwave-safe bowl or heavy nonaluminum pot, stir the water and sugar together until dissolved, then add the plums, cover tightly with plastic wrap or a lid, and microwave on high (100 percent) for 15 minutes or bring to a boil over medium heat and then simmer for 12 to 20 minutes. Cool for 30 minutes.

Ladle a small amount of the plums and their liquid into a strainer set over a large bowl. Press firmly on the plums to extract all of their liquid, but not so hard that the flesh pushes through the strainer. Discard the skins and pulp, and repeat with the remaining plums. Add the lemon juice, taste, and add a little more sugar if you wish.

Can be refrigerated for 2 to 3 days or frozen for up to 3 months.

FRESH STAR FRUIT AND HONEY SAUCE

With their gentle, tropical flavor, star fruit make a light dessert sauce that is elegant, graceful, and a hint exotic.

Serve with fresh fruits or spoon over light homemade cakes, or pass with fresh fruit salads. At breakfast, serve with pancakes, waffles, or French toast.

Makes about 1 ½ cups

6 large ripe (tender) star fruits, cut into
    1- to 2-inch chunks
2 tablespoons honey

In a food processor, combine the star fruit and honey and purée until smooth. Serve at room temperature.

FRESH RASPBERRY PURÉE

Made with fresh or frozen berries, purées are a simple and popular way to make a dessert sauce. The raspberry has a medium-thick texture and a rich berry flavor, even when frozen berries are used.

Serve with all kinds of cakes, from a light lemon layer cake to a rich dark chocolate cake, with fresh or poached fruit, or use for breakfast atop pancakes or French toast.

Makes about 2 cups

> 1 pint fresh raspberries (frozen, drained
> raspberries can be substituted)
> Juice of ¼ small lemon
> About 1 tablespoon sugar, if needed

Process the raspberries and lemon juice in a food processor for about 30 seconds to make a fine purée. Taste, and add sugar if needed. Purée again until sugar is melted.

Push through a strainer for a finely textured sauce; otherwise pour into a jar, cover, and refrigerate until needed.

Fresh Strawberry Purée

Substitute fresh strawberries for the raspberries and add the juice of ½ orange instead of the lemon juice.

Fresh Blackberry Purée, Fresh Blueberry Purée, or Fresh Mulberry Purée

Substitute fresh (or frozen drained) blackberries, fresh blueberries, or fresh mulberries for the raspberries.

Mango Pineapple Purée

Substitute 2 very ripe mangoes, peeled and cut off the seed, for the raspberries and substitute ¼ cup pineapple juice for the lemon juice.

DRIED CHERRY SAUCE

Made with dried fruits, these sauces have a darker color and a more intense flavor that the fresh fruit puree sauces. A large variety of dried fruits are available in health and whole-foods markets, so experiment with your favorites. These are particularly good sauces to make in winter, when ripe fresh fruits are sometimes in short supply.

Serve over cakes and puddings, or under or alongside fresh or poached fruits. At breakfast, use to top pancakes, waffles, or French toast. Also excellent on bread puddings or hot cereals.

Makes about 2 cups

1 cup hot tapwater
¼ cup sugar
1 cup dried Bing or sweetened sour cherries

In a small saucepan, bring the water and sugar to a boil over high heat, stirring a few times to dissolve the sugar. Add the cherries and simmer, uncovered, until very tender, about 8 minutes.

Purée in a food processor until a fine sauce forms, about 30 seconds. Because some dried fruits are drier and sweeter than others (buy the most moist fruits when you can), it may be necessary to adjust the texture by adding a little water or apple juice to thin the sauce, and to adjust the sweetness by adding a little more sugar.

Pour into a jar, cover, and refrigerate until needed.

Dried Blueberry Sauce, Dried Cranberry Sauce, Dried Banana Sauce, or Dried Star Fruit Sauce

Substitute dried blueberries, dried cranberries, dried bananas, or star fruit for the cherries.

Dried Mission Fig Sauce or Dried Italian Plum Sauce

Substitute ¾ cup diced, dried mission figs or prunes for the cherries.

STRAWBERRY ESSENCE

Just defrost, strain, and chill to make these intensely colored, translucent sauces that have the deepest of berry flavors.

Makes about 1½ to 2 cups

**3 packages, about 10 ounces each,
frozen strawberries in syrup**

Defrost the berries completely. Pour into a strainer and let drain completely, pressing only very gently on the pulp to extract its juice, but not so hard that any purée is accidentally pushed through the strainer.

Refrigerate in a covered jar until needed.

Raspberry Essence, Blueberry Essence, or Dark Cherry Essence

Substitute raspberries, blueberries, or dark cherries for the strawberries.

Three-Berry Essence

Use 1 package each of frozen blueberries in syrup, frozen blackberries in syrup, and frozen raspberries in syrup.

HONEY LEMON SAUCE

This clear, honey and lemon–flavored sauce takes only seconds to make.

Serve over light cakes, like angel food; with fresh fruit over heavier cakes, like pound cake; or use with fresh fruits or fruit salads. At breakfast, pour on pancakes, waffles, or French toast.

Makes about 1¼ cups

½ cup light corn syrup
½ cup honey
Juice of ½ large lemon
¼ cup water

Whisk everything together. Can be refrigerated, tightly covered, for up to 3 days or frozen for up to 3 months.

Maple Syrup Sauce

Substitute maple syrup for the honey and 1 teaspoon vanilla for the lemon juice.

Red Wine Dessert Sauce

The flavors in this deep burgundy-colored sauce are intensely concentrated, so use it sparingly.

Serve with fresh fruits, especially tropical fruits like pineapple, papaya, and mango; with poached fruits, like pears; or use as a dipping sauce for large fresh strawberries.

Makes about 1 cup

1 750-ml bottle fruity red wine
2- to 3-inch cinnamon stick, broken
  into a few pieces
¼-inch slice of an orange

¼-inch slice of a lemon
1-inch chunk fresh gingerroot, peeled and
  cut into a few pieces
1 cup sugar

Bring everything to a boil over medium heat, stirring occasionally until the sugar dissolves. Boil until reduced to 1 cup, about 25 to 30 minutes.

Appendix

......

Food List with
Suggested Sauces

Beef

Breakfast Foods

Casseroles

Enchiladas and Tapas

Fruit Toppings

Game

Lamb

Pasta

Pork

Poultry

Risotto/Polenta

Salads

Salad Dressings

Sandwiches

Seafood

Snacks and Dips
(including cold vegetables)

Soups

Stews

Tex-Mex Dishes

Vegetables (including baked potatoes)

BEEF

BREAKFAST FOODS

Fresh Apple Chutney   23

Pear and Red Wine Chutney   25

Dried Apricot, Currant, and Orange Gremolata   36

Dried Blueberry, Lemon, and Candied Pineapple Gremolata   37

Dried Cherry and Cranberry Gremolata   38

Fresh Pineapple Orange Spice Sauce   123

Fresh Damson Plum Sauce   124

Fresh Star Fruit and Honey Sauce   125

Fresh Raspberry Purée   126

Honey Lemon Sauce   129

CASSEROLES

White Bean Sauce   8

Marinara Sauce   57

Light Sour Cream "Mayonnaise"   94

Hot Green Pepper Sauce   105

ENCHILADAS AND TAPAS

Green Bell Pepper and Dill Relish   31

Cilantro and Jalapeño Gremolata   33

Fresh Tomato Salsa   47

FRUIT TOPPINGS

Dried Apricot, Currant, and Orange Gremolata   36

Dried Blueberry, Lemon, and Candied Pineapple Gremolata   37

Dried Cherry and Cranberry Gremolata   38

Honeydew and Tomatillo Salsa   42

Fresh Pineapple Orange Spice Sauce   123

Fresh Damson Plum Sauce   124

Fresh Star Fruit and Honey Sauce   125

Fresh Raspberry Purée   126

Dried Cherry Sauce   127

Strawberry Essence   128

Honey Lemon Sauce   129

Red Wine Dessert Sauce   130

GAME

Forest Mushroom Sauce   11

Fresh Mango Salsa   43

Extra-Easy Sundried Tomato Sauce   61

Chicken Demiglaze Sauce   83

Anise-Flavored Marinade and Dipping Sauce   111

Korean Marinade and Dipping Sauce   113

Moroccan-Style Marinade and Dipping Sauce   115

Tropp-Inspired Marinade and Dipping Sauce   119

Fresh Damson Plum Sauce   124

LAMB

White Bean Aioli   7

Traditional Italian Green Sauce   9

Sesame-Scented Lentil Sauce   10

Forest Mushroom Sauce   11

Poblano and Green Bell Pepper Sauce with Mint   14

Red Pepper Sofrito   16

PASTA

Asparagus Sauce   3

Black Bean, Tomato, and Dill Sauce   5

Pale Pink Bean Sauce   6

White Bean Sauce   8

Sesame-Scented Lentil Sauce   10

Mushroom and Eggplant Sauce with Tomatoes and Herbs   12

Jean-Louis Palladin's Incredible Onion Sauce   13

Poblano and Green Bell Pepper Sauce with Mint   14

Red Pepper Sofrito   16

A Very Light Tomato Sauce with Chickpeas   53

Fresh Tomato Couli   55

Marinara Sauce   57

Puttanesca Sauce   58

Raw Tomato Concassée   59

Fresh Italian Ragu   60

Yellow Pepper Tomato Sauce   64

PORK

Black Bean, Tomato, and Dill Sauce   5

Traditional Italian Green Sauce   9

Forest Mushroom Sauce   11

Poblano and Green Bell Pepper Sauce with Mint   14

Green Pepper Sofrito   17

A Sprightly Tomatillo Sauce   18

Wasabi Mustard Sauce   19

Fresh Apple Chutney   23

Holiday Three-Berry and Beet Chutney   24

Pear and Red Wine Chutney   25

POULTRY

Honey Mustard Dressing with Balsamic Vinegar   71

Russian Dressing   73

Chicken Demiglaze Sauce   83

Lightly Minted Cucumber Sauce   89

My Grandmother's Fresh Dill and Mint Sauce   90

Light Sour Cream "Mayonnaise"   94

Two-Mustard Sauce   95

Basil Barbeque Sauce   99

Southwestern-Style Dried Chili Sauce   101

Jamaican Jerk Barbeque and Basting Sauce   102

Midwestern Barbeque Sauce   103

Hot Yellow Pepper Sauce with Saffron   106

Rouille   107

Texas Barbeque Sauce   108

Honey Mustard Marinade and Dipping Sauce   112

Moroccan-Style Marinade and Dipping Sauce   115

Tandoori Marinade and Dipping Sauce   117

Teriyaki Marinade and Dipping Sauce   118

Tropp-Inspired Marinade and Dipping Sauce   119

Fresh Damson Plum Sauce   124

RISOTTO/POLENTA

Black Bean Sauce with Mild Green Chilies   4

Mushroom and Eggplant Sauce with Tomatoes and Herbs   12

Red Pepper Sofrito   16

Green Pepper Sofrito   17

Parsley, Tarragon, Red Onion, and Lemon Gremolata   35

SALADS

Asparagus Sauce   3

Poblano and Green Bell Pepper Sauce with Mint   14

My Grandmother's Fresh Dill and Mint Sauce   90

Miso Saffron Sauce   96

SALAD DRESSINGS

Creamy Avocado Lime Dressing   67

Beet and Raspberry Vinegar Dressing   68

Chickpea and Sherry Vinegar Dressing   69

Green Goddess Dressing   70

Honey Mustard Dressing with Balsamic Vinegar   71

Miso Lemon Dressing   72

Russian Dressing   73

Thousand Island Dressing   75

My Grandmother's Fresh Dill and Mint Sauce   90

Light Sour Cream "Mayonnaise"   94

SANDWICHES

Black Bean, Tomato, and Dill Sauce   5

White Bean Aioli   7

Traditional Italian Green Sauce   9

Mushroom and Eggplant Sauce with Tomatoes and Herbs   12

Wasabi Mustard Sauce   19

Holiday Three-Berry and Beet Chutney   24

Red Cabbage and Raspberry Chutney   26

Many Vegetable Chutney   27

SEAFOOD

SNACKS AND DIPS *(including cold vegetables)*

SOUPS

Pale Pink Bean Sauce   6

White Bean Aioli   7

Sesame-Scented Lentil Sauce   10

Red Pepper Sofrito   16

Green Pepper Sofrito   17

Many Vegetable Chutney   27

Cilantro and Jalapeño Gremolata   33

Two-Mustard Sauce   95

Rouille   107

STEWS

Pale Pink Bean Sauce   6

Sesame-Scented Lentil Sauce   10

Red Pepper Sofrito   16

Green Pepper Sofrito   17

Many Vegetable Chutney   27

Cilantro and Jalapeño Gremolata   33

Green Peppercorn and Dill Gremolata   34

Parsley, Tarragon, Red Onion, and Lemon Gremolata   35

Hot Green Pepper Sauce   105

Hot Yellow Pepper Sauce with Saffron   106

Rouille   107

TEX-MEX DISHES

Black Bean Sauce with Mild Green Chilies   4

The Best-Ever Tomato Salsa   46

Fresh Tomato Salsa with Avocado   48

VEGETABLES (including baked potatoes)

Asparagus Sauce   3

Black Bean Sauce with Mild Green Chilies   4

Pale Pink Bean Sauce   6

White Bean Aioli   7

White Bean Sauce   8

Traditional Italian Green Sauce   9

Sesame-Scented Lentil Sauce   10

Jean-Louis Palladin's Incredible Onion Sauce   13

Poblano and Green Bell Pepper Sauce with Mint   14

Roasted Red Pepper Purée with Orange and Dill   15

Holiday Three-Berry and Beet Chutney   24

Red Cabbage and Raspberry Chutney   26

Sweet-and-Sour Corn Relish   29

Fresh Tomato Salsa with Avocado   48

Yellow Tomato and Ginger Salsa   49

Marinara Sauce   57

Raw Tomato Concassée   59

Fresh Italian Ragu   60

Extra-Easy Sundried Tomato Sauce   61

Yellow Pepper Tomato Sauce   64

Beet and Raspberry Vinegar Dressing   68

Honey Mustard Dressing with Balsamic Vinegar   71

My Grandmother's Fresh Dill and Mint Sauce   90

Emerald Green Sauce   91

Horseradish Cream Sauce   93

Light Sour Cream "Mayonnaise"   94

Two-Mustard Sauce   95

Hot Yellow Pepper Sauce with Saffron   106

Index